THE #1 MARKETING GUIDE FOR COSMETIC AND PLASTIC SURGEONS

FULLY BOOKED

TOP Marketing Secrets REVEALED to Dominate & Own Your Cosmetic Surgery Market

Learn How Top Plastic Surgeons Are Capturing More Leads & Closing More Surgery Bookings

HUYEN TRUONG

www.queenofcosmeticmarketing.com

(Division of Online Marketing For Doctors)

Paperback ISBN: 978-0-646-81952-5

eBook ISBN: 978-0-646-81970-9

Audio book ISBN: 978-0-6489512-0-9

FOREWORD

Dear Cosmetic and Plastic Surgeons,

As I know how time-poor you are, I'll keep this book really short.

After reading this book, or listening to the audio version, you'll have a clearer road map of how to completely **dominate and own** your cosmetic marketing market.

My book will give you a clear picture of how you can position yourself as *the* choice, not just a choice in your cosmetic surgery market. Once you know how to position yourself as *the choice*... patients will come running to you.

This book will give you a high-level strategy for the direction that you need to go in, in order to be a celebrity authority in your niche.

Unlike most books on marketing that focus on just one channel or one strategy, I didn't want to give you just one tactic that only worked today, and maybe not tomorrow. I wanted to give you a framework that you could use to get new patients from any channel; today, tomorrow, and forever.

I'll leave the best tools that you need to equip your business with in the "Make Your Life Easier" bonus section of this book, and you can assign those parts to other team members if you don't have the time yourself. And if you don't have any other people to help you with this material, I'll also show you how to find some great help too.

This book will help you get to where you want to go. Faster.

Huyen Truong, MBA

Queen of Cosmetic Marketing

Division of Online Marketing For Doctors

Huyen Truong

CONTENTS

MY BACKGROUND

"The number of requests for consultations has at least doubled in the last 5 months, which is a very good sign. We're very impressed with how much detail Online Marketing For Doctors put into the plan, their projections, and what they might be able to achieve for us. I've enjoyed working with both principles. We look forward to the future, as right now the present is very positive for us."

-DR. DARRYL HODGKINSON,
MBBS (Honors II) FRCS (C), FACS, FACCS,
Cosmetic & Plastic/Reconstructive Surgeon

Now, before we get started... a quick introduction. My name is Huyen Truong, and I am the founder and director of Queen of Cosmetic Marketing (www.queenofcosmeticmarketing.com) a division of Online Marketing For Doctors - a marketing agency that specialises in patient generation for cosmetic and plastic surgeons around the world.

You can learn more about my journey and my agency in my Author's Biography.

Hearing the term "marketing agency" brings scepticism, raised eyebrows, and even frustration day in and day out from my clients.

They've been sold on the same old marketing techniques, and many have already tried and failed five - or even six - different agencies, struggling to find the right partner to help them grow their business.

And I understand why it would have been difficult to find that right partner. Those agencies don't have a clue about the cosmetic surgery industry.

I understand the frustration.

I understand the doubts.

I understand the concerns.

Because of my industry experience, what I can offer is different in both approach and results.

At the heart of it, there are two types of surgeons that win their market: price-driven surgeons and celebrity surgeons.

Price-driven surgeons compete based on price, but it's not always sustainable. All it takes is someone more aggressive entering the market to erode any gains that you have achieved.

Celebrity, or expert, surgeons work for years, making gains that last, as they become an authority on particular procedures. This requires a combination of experience and targeted marketing.

When you're an expert, patients seek you out. The patient-surgeon relationship starts out with an essential ingredient: trust. And no amount of advertising spent can buy a potential patient's trust.

I notice a lot of practices trying the same old marketing tactics, and they end up looking the same as they did before. If you search in

Google any procedure keywords right now, you will see a bunch of ads from different practices screaming out the same type of message, hoping that they can cut through the noise, rise above the water, and stand out.

If you try the same marketing techniques as any other surgeon, you will have the same results.

To be honest, working in the hyper-competitive digital marketing industry, I myself needed to discover the secret to marketing success and setting myself apart from my competitors as much as my clients have to.

I knew I needed to change the traditional marketing strategy; find a new path that would allow me and the clients I represent, to achieve incredible gains regardless of the competition that we were up against.

So, I went out and I did just that.

And it worked!

After one year of applying the 6 secrets that I detail in this book, my business' growth skyrocketed by 166%.

That's why I am writing this book for you—to share with you what I've learnt from my own experience helping many plastic and cosmetic surgeons from around the world achieve incredible growth in their businesses. This book will…

- …teach you how to generate more patients and revenue from your marketing activities.

- ...show you how you can become a celebrity authority in your cosmetic surgery category without needing a massive PR budget and decades of experience.

There are six secrets contained in this book that I'm about to reveal to you. Each is a key element to achieving the sustainable long-term gains that you're looking for in your practice.

Are you ready to go on a journey that you'll have wished that you had started earlier?

But... before we get going with these 6 incredible secrets, we need to make sure that you are ready, and that your practice is set up properly.

HAVING THE RIGHT MINDSET

Have you listened to Brian Tracy – a legendary leadership and personal development coach?

He has some incredibly valuable books and YouTube videos online. If you haven't listened to Brian Tracy, please do.

He famously said:

"You are not in the business you think you are in—you are in the ***marketing business.****"*

When I first heard that years ago, I thought... *oh my goodness!* My agency was just starting out, and I was specializing in SEO services at that time. And so I naturally thought that I was in the SEO business.

In reality, SEO was just my service. I was in the business of marketing my skills as a Search Marketing Strategist, convincing people that I could help get their websites to rank better on Google.

One of the most important abilities of any practice owner is **to be able to market and sell their services, products, and solutions** to your patients or referring partners.

I really want to emphasize this—**you are in the marketing business.**

It doesn't mean that your surgical skills are not important. You still need to have great clinical skills so that when patients come in, they have a good experience with your clinic and they rave about you later.

But you need to have that ability to market and attract new patients.

Just waiting around and relying on word of mouth or referrals (which I do love by the way) is not scalable, as you won't know when your next patient is coming in. You can't make plans around that level of uncertainty.

If you are not good at marketing, then someone else out there who is more aggressive with their marketing tactics, regardless of their skillset, is going to get the lion's share of the market.

Marketing is the number one ability that you need to have.

Please stop for a second and think about the big names in your industry right now. What names pop into your head?

What do you think is the **one thing** that they all have **in common?**

They are probably **all great marketers.**

COMMON MISTAKES

One of the most common mistakes made by a lot of practices when it comes to developing a digital marketing strategy is that they don't think about their overall marketing strategy. A high-level overarching strategy that informs all of their marketing efforts to come.

We know that a lot of digital marketing agencies will start with questions like "What keywords do you want to rank for?", when they first start discussing marketing strategy with a client, and they'll start making technical changes on your website based on those answers without even thinking about a long-term, high-level marketing strategy that could take a practice to the next level.

You may have even experienced this process in the agencies that you've worked with in the past.

You need to have a completely different approach when it comes to your digital marketing efforts than a quick-fix keyword ranking approach.

Instead, start by looking at the foundational elements of all marketing (both traditional and digital) activities—**Market Segment & Market Positioning.**

"Your wealth is in direct proportion with how well you know your target market."

HUYEN TRUONG

MARKET POSITIONING THE KEY STEP THAT IS OFTEN MISSED

Do you know that the most valuable currency in the world is attention?

More eyeballs on you, more traffic, more enquiries, and more sales.

It has never been easier to reach your dream prospect. But it's never been harder to get, keep, and leverage their attention.

That's why all of those entertainment, media and sporting celebrities try very hard (and sometimes to the extreme) to get, keep and leverage our attention. Your goal is not so dissimilar to that, in that you want to be a celebrity authority.

Now...I'm not talking about a celebrity like Kim Kardashian.

I'm talking about the celebrity authority in your niche. Although, if that's what you want, go for it! All the more power to you!

Me Too - I'm a plastic surgeon

Me Better – I'm an expert

Me Only – I'm *the* celebrity authority

Do you see the differences in those three categories?

When you are an expert, people know about your expertise, obviously. People call you and they want to do business with you.

But when you are the celebrity authority in your niche, you are the go-to person. A category king or queen – the celebrity authority in a niche - is the go-to person for prospects seeking advice or help when the market has become crowded and saturated.

When you are a celebrity authority, people are happy even if they just get to *meet* you.

Do you see the distinction? They are happy that they have FINALLY gotten to you, and they will pay whatever you ask to be treated by you. From the patient's perspective, you are the celebrity authority.

When you have that sort of power, prospective patients and money finds you. You will never be out of money.

Don't you want that?

Do you want to completely own and dominate your category or niche?

One time, I met a coach at a conference and I asked him… "What are you working on now?". He replied, "I am a success coach, I help people become more successful."

I replied, "Oh ok, interesting...and what area do you specialise in?"

"Any area! I help people with finance, business, relationships, and weight loss. If they have issues with their confidence, I can help them boost that too."

Don't you find this scenario familiar?

It's so broad and wide, and I personally just don't get it. If you use that generalist approach with your marketing, people will think that you are a "jack of all trades"—and a master of none.

People want to buy from a specialist, not a generalist.

Are you with me on this?

Imagine that you go to see a general dentist, and they suddenly say, "Hmmm…you seem to have an uneven bump on your nose. You know I can get some filler to even it out.". And then later they say, "Um, look at the way you sit. I think you may have a back problem. After this, why don't you turn around and let me crack your back?".

What are you going to do? You'd run, right? But somehow it is still happening in many businesses today. This jack-of-all-trades mentally towards marketing still exists; "I can fix any appearance problems—eyes, nose, breast, tummy, hip—from your toes right to the top of your head. You name it! Whatever you want!".

Does this approach look familiar to any of the surgeons reading this book?

Figure 1: General messages like these don't build authority; there is no positioning in place

I like niches. If you play in a field that has too much competition, then everything will be driven by price, which will bring down your profit margin.

But if you stay in your own lane, and become the celebrity king or queen of your niche, your marketing costs will lower over time, and your margins will be higher and you can scale more easily.

So, how do you become the go-to celebrity authority in your niche?

You need to focus on your positioning and your message consistency with your target audience; delivering a consistent, clear message to one group of people ONLY. Educate them, and entertain them so they will like and trust you, buying from you without any further consideration.

When you cater your content and message to one group of people, it will be more relevant and capture your target audience's attention better than some general message.

Be laser-focused with your target market; is it 30–45-year-old mothers with kids, retired seniors, or young women in their 20s who love to do selfies and post pictures of themselves on Instagram?

Why do we get this laser-focused? Because it will be easier for you to identify and understand their problems, frustrations, pain points, preferences, desires, and even the language that they use, better than anyone else and for tailoring your marketing message to them.

Your identified target market will feel like you are one of them, that you understand them, and that's how you can connect with them; opening their hearts and their wallets.

Some of you will ask; "I have different services and procedures that I offer, how can I focus on one thing, or just one audience?".

You can always offer other services or solutions, but when it comes to your outbound marketing messages and the content that you are pushing out, it should only serve that specific target audience.

Your goal is to be the go-to celebrity authority surgeon for that target audience. Then you can provide a whole list of services to that market once they have connected with you.

Remember: The amount of money you make will depend on **how well you know your target market.**

Please write this down.

"The riches are in the niches."

You need to be crystal clear with your marketing efforts. Who do you serve? Focus on something that you are the best at.

Choosing a niche doesn't mean choosing one forever. It simply means focusing on something that you are good at, that you have a great passion for right NOW. You can always switch later. But focusing on a niche is important at any time.

"When you speak to everyone,
you speak to no one."

MEREDITH HILL

MARKET SEGMENTATION
CLEARLY DEFINE YOUR TARGET AUDIENCE

"Who is your typical ideal patient?" – that is one of the first questions that I often ask plastic surgeons when I first talk to them. I usually get a common answer; "We target pretty much anyone who wants to get some cosmetic surgery done.".

Do you see a problem here?

As marketing Hall of Famer Seth Godin once famously said; "Everyone is not your customer.".

You need to figure out **WHO** your target patient is. **WHAT** they want so badly that they will give up anything to get it, and then go **TELL** them how you can help...**in their language.**

To better identify your target audience, there are a handful of unique qualifiers focused on age range, gender, lifestyles, and primary medical concerns. To focus on lead generation, you will also need to identify the common characteristics of these ideal patients, which we refer to as personas.

Once we have clearly identified each of these ideal patient personas, all of your communications will be crafted to appeal to their interests and desires.

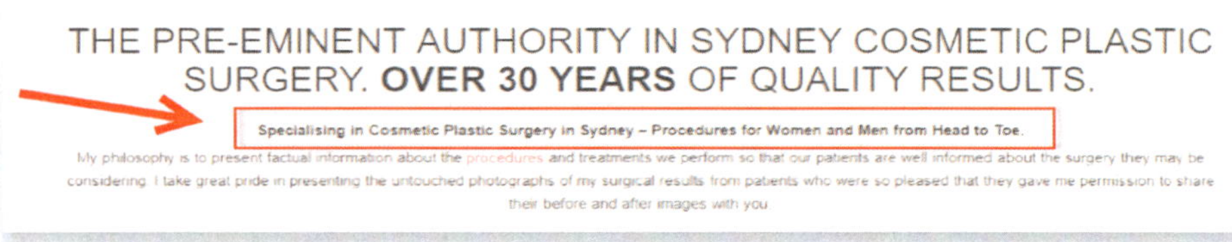

Figure 2: This sentence signals a marketing strategy designed to appeal to anyone and everyone

For example, Brooke is a happily married 55-year-old bank manager who lives in the wealthier eastern suburbs of Sydney, Australia. Now that her children have left the nest, Brooke has more time for herself and for enjoying life a bit more; like travelling overseas with her husband and friends.

She has been contemplating recently whether she should try cosmetic surgery for removing some of the signs of aging from around her face.

She doesn't feel comfortable with the pulled stretched look that she's seen from other people's facelifts, fearing she'd end up with a similar look. Instead, she'd prefer something that her friends and family would think that she still looks like herself, just more youthful, refreshed, and vibrant!

The marketing approach here is to try to determine how best we can begin a conversation with Brooke, and other women like her.

By understanding the likes, dislikes, and habits of these women we can then craft advertisements, copy for landing pages, videos, and social media messages that address them at a personal level, appealing to their unique challenges and desires.

Developing personas is very important to the success of any marketing strategy, and it is crucial for successfully attracting qualified leads to your cosmetic surgery practice.

Once you identify your target audience's detailed persona, including their pains and desires in detail, what you need to do next is to figure out where they are spending their time online for sending them targeted messages.

THE DREAM 100 LIST FOR YOUR CLINIC

I was introduced to the concept of the "Dream 100" when I was reading one of the current best-selling digital marketing books called Traffic Secrets by Russell Brunson; which is the idea of identifying the top 100 tribes that thousands of your target audience are already active members of and finding a way to infiltrate these tribe members for displaying your targeted message to these tribe members. And then this will take our ideal buyers from "I've never heard of this clinic?" to "What is this clinic I keep hearing about?".

The goal of this exercise is to find out where these dream patients are hiding. If you don't truly understand your dream patients, then it will be harder to find them. But if you really understand them, then you should already know where they're congregating.

One time, Russell was at an event in Puerto Rico, and he had a chance to spend time with Rachel Hollis, the author of the *#1 New York Times* bestseller *Girl, Wash Your Face*. He asked her the secrets of selling over a million copies of her books, and she told him;

> *We asked ourselves this question: "What are the tribes that my women are already in? What Facebook groups, what Instagram channels, what hashtags are they following?" After we identified these things, we tried to figure out who the tribe owners of these women were. Who do we need to become friends with? Anyone who had over 200,000 followers, we would direct message (DM) them, tell them who we were, and ask them if we could talk. We started messaging everyone. Our focus was to find the tribes and then figure out the best ways to infiltrate them.*

That is the Dream 100 method! She didn't call it that, but that's *exactly* what she had done to quickly become one of the best-selling authors of all time.

At this point, some of you may be thinking… "But Huyen, I'm not selling a book or a product online. I'm a local brick-and-mortar business trying to generate local leads online!". Don't worry, this strategy still works, even though you will need to look at it a little differently.

When building your Dream 100 list, instead of identifying the national influencers or leaders in your niche, you need to identify your local influencers. This concept works for my business and every business. Period.

In order to find out where these ideal dream patients are congregating online, here are some questions that you should be asking yourself:

- What are the top websites that my dream patients visit?
- What forums or message boards do they participate in?

- What magazines do they flip through?
- What Facebook groups are they engaged in?
- Who are the influencers that they follow on Facebook and Instagram?
- What podcasts do they listen to?
- What are the email newsletters that they are subscribed to?
- What blogs do they read?
- What channels are they following on YouTube?
- What keywords are they using in Google or YouTube searches to find information?

Answering these questions will help you to start identifying where your dream patient personas are residing. Once you know where they're congregating online, it's pretty easy to put your targeted messages and hooks in front of them, which I am going to show you shortly, for pulling them into your sales funnels.

By doing this exercise, you'll be able to reach your targeted audience directly through the relationship that we have created with the owner of these tribes, producing a much more effective Return On Investment than simple mass media targeting.

SET-UP & BUILD AUTHORITY WITH YOUR TARGET AUDIENCE

Once you know who your target audience is, it is time to set up and build authority with that target audience, so that you can become the celebrity authority in this niche.

Your CAE Factors

First, patients don't invest in high-priced procedures from just any old Dr Nobody. Instead, I have seen that they go to Dr CAE.

In order for someone to pay you market-leading rates, you are going to have to become a "somebody". But how do you do this without waiting on gaining 20 years of experience to become established?

Life is far too short for that, so let me introduce you to the CAE factor.

- Celebrity
- Authority
- Expertise

As the old adage goes; all other things being equal, people buy from other people that they know, like, and trust. As Dan S. Kennedy, known as the godfather of direct marketing, succinctly put it:

"If you aren't deliberately, systematically, methodically—or rapidly and dramatically—establishing yourself as a celebrity, at least to your clientele and target market, you're asleep at the wheel, ignoring what is fuelling the entire economy around you, and neglecting the development of a measurably valuable asset."

The question is:

Do you have a plan that you are following to make yourself a (bigger) celebrity?

If not, why not? If not now, when?

If you are keen, please keep reading, as I'm about to show you a step-by-step plan to become a celebrity authority in your niche.

What Are the CAE Factor's Effects?

During the height of Kim Kardashian's celebrity appeal, she was commanding nearly $1 million for her public appearances.

Forbes said Kardashian "has monetized fame better than any other."

She is, perhaps, the ultimate example of cashing in on being famous for doing nothing.

The good news is that you don't have to be a Kardashian to manufacture that same celebrity vibe.

Whew!

Professionally, you've written papers for journals and gained promotions and certifications to enhance your status. You've trained for years to perfect your craft. You're a medical professional with years of training.

That's a great start!

Expertise? Check.

Authority? Check.

All that's missing is the celebrity.

Easy to say, but how do you establish it?

Having the complete CAE factor will put you further ahead of your competition. You'll become a hot commodity for those looking for the services that you offer. And when you're a hot commodity, you can keep your prices at a level that works for you, while still maintaining a stream of patients seeking you out.

Developing that celebrity component of your CAE factor becomes vitally important. And developing your CAE factor is so simple that you may not believe how easy it can be at first.

It would seem difficult, a solution that only a few very lucky ones have inadvertently stumbled upon and had the luxury to take advantage of. But the reality is, this isn't that difficult, and the "secret" solution was out there waiting for you to take advantage of it, all this time.

Drawing on my own expertise, I've condensed this solution into 6 easy actionable "secret" steps that anyone wanting to become the celebrity authority in their niche can do.

You've got the power in you to take charge and change your practice's future today. Just turn the page.

SECRET #1: BECOME A PUBLISHED AUTHOR

Write a book? Really? *Boy… did we get off on the wrong foot!*

This idea may sound slightly unorthodox, but it really works! You can do it, and it can transform your marketing tactics and make your practice more successful because of it.

I understand if you're hesitant. But this isn't some vanity publishing exercise that will result in something that nobody wants to read. Follow my advice, and people will read your book, and it will directly generate you more new patients.

Having your own published book is at the very heart of helping you compete, and separating you from other generic surgeons, and it helps build your authority and further demonstrates your expertise. And I'm going to reveal to you how easily we can transform you into a successful published author, including how you can leverage the benefits that publishing can give you to set yourself apart from your competition and generate more new quality patients.

A book is like a stone thrown into a pond. It creates a ripple effect.

For example, I've used books before to reach out to my personal audience of cosmetic and plastic surgeons such as yourself. My hope is that they will reach out to me, and seek my help as a result.

I didn't have to ask, instead, surgeons reached out because I'd shown them that I understood their market, and I've shown them how to get ahead in it.

Essentially, I'm asking you to do what I do. I wouldn't do it if it didn't work for me. Books give useful information, and this will earn respect and gain trust among your audience.

With my published material, people have found my information useful, so they turn to me when they need advice. I may have simply gained respect. I may one day gain a referral. But it's an important step in building credibility.

This book isn't *just* about marketing strategies: it's a real-life example of how this strategy works.

The 5 Key Benefits of Publishing a Book

1. Trust and credibility

The goal isn't simply to get rich from book sales, although that would be nice. If anything, I'd advise you to give away free copies of your book!

What actually makes you rich, is the trust and credibility that results from being the author of a well-written, helpful book.

Prospective patients, reading your future book will help them to learn exactly how you can help them. You will instantly gain that CAE factor that we discussed earlier because an author is an authority.

A cosmetic or plastic surgeon who is also an author is unique. You will find only a handful of books about cosmetic surgery that are aimed at consumers rather than practitioners. Join these elite few and establish yourself as an authority in your niche.

2. Recognition

With your book in circulation, the media may start to contact you, sensing that you could provide valuable insight into stories that they are working on. That type of media attention is invaluable, helping to increase your name recognition, but also building up your celebrity profile.

But that isn't all… your peers could start inviting you to speak at conferences and conventions, further enhancing your reputation. Referring physicians will begin to know your name in the industry, and take you more seriously, even before they've met you.

A book can open doors for you.

3. Patient conversion

Books aren't meant to boost your ego—they are meant to boost your patient numbers.

Let's think about your current website:

- Website traffic; how many visits do you get per month?
- Conversion rate; and how many of those make an enquiry?
- Consultations; and how many enquiries come in for an initial consultation?
- Sales; and then finally…how many consultations will undergo treatment?

The journey from initial interest to becoming a patient can break down at each step, and in many different ways, and you can use your book to fix those breakdowns. Not in every case, but sufficiently enough to make a real difference to your business.

Imagine a scenario in which you're advising a patient about her desires around having breast augmentation surgery, and the risks and benefits involved.

She may not be 100% convinced. As she leaves you can offer her a complimentary copy of your book, mentioning that other patients had found the book helpful in working through their thoughts.

That interaction has helped you win her trust and position yourself as an authority. The book can produce trust and credibility. It could be the element that wipes away lingering doubts that they may have. That's a powerful mix and a winning formula.

4. Prospecting with Amazon

Your book is more than a conversion tool—it's also a prospecting tool.

I'll show you later in this section how powerful your book can be when it is used to generate prospects online, but right now I want you to use your book to harness the power of Amazon in the form of online visibility and trust.

When someone is uncertain about something, they usually ask for help. They may ask a friend, a colleague, or even a specialist. These days, people are just as likely to look online.

The written word is a trusted source of information. And where do you look for books online? Our good friend Amazon. People often search for information on Amazon.

It's almost irrelevant whether or not they buy the book, as what matters is that the book can be found there, bringing awareness to you, and your practice. It will make a difference with your credibility. And increased credibility brings more enquiries.

5. Protecting your reputation

Obviously, a book can build your reputation. But there are less obvious, but just as important, ways that a book can also protect it.

It's common to receive an occasional bad review online, most practices will. You may also be painfully aware of how a bad review can spoil the good reviews that you have.

We'll talk about building your reputation online later. Let's talk about protecting your reputation.

Before publishing your book, external third-party review sites are one of the first things to pop up in search engine results. But doing the same search after you've published your book; the search results will be flooded with your website, your social media profiles, your Amazon listing, and press reviews of your book, pushing those third-party sites further down the list.

First impressions matter. By having a published book appearing in rankings, even before your prospective patients have a chance to see the occasional bad review, they will know that you are an expert in your field, a widely respected author, and a celebrity authority figure.

That sort of protection will help take the sting out of any negative reviews still lurking out there.

How to Publish Your Book – 12 Easy Steps

See? Not so madcap after all.

This genuine, highly effective strategy will set you apart and win you more patients.

But of course, I've heard the objections before… "How am I expected to find the time to write a book in the first place?". Would you believe me if I told you that you can become a published author in as little as five hours.

Five. Hours. Read on.

Of course, you'll need a little help from your practice manager or secretary or a virtual assistant (I'll show you how to find a great one in the bonus chapter).

You will also need a few special online tools, but it is achievable, you just need the right approach.

The goal is *not* to write about yourself, that is a common writing mistake.

- All about *me*.
- How *I* can help you.
- This is what *I* do.
- *I* do it this way.

Your book is going to be different. It needs to be written from your average prospective patient's point of view. The book needs to address their questions and concerns.

- What's in it for *them*?
- What will *they* learn from the book?
- What's the best decision for *them*?

Your book will become a spectacular resource without ever having to market it as such, all by answering your patient's concerns.

Writing a book in five hours or less is easier than you might think, and you can do it, and I've got a simple 12 step formula below to prove it.

Let's get started.

Step #1: Choose Your Procedure

Your book should focus on only one procedure. This will help your book to find its ideal market and help establish your reputation in a particular niche.

Don't go for general "cosmetic surgery" topics, which I see all too frequently on Amazon. This sort of broad topic won't cut through the broad range of general cosmetic surgery books out there or get you the right type of prospective patients.

Step #2: Profile Your Patient

Next, I want you to profile your typical patient, by answering the following questions about who they are and what their persona is;

- Are they male or female?
- How old is your ideal patient?
- Where do they live?
- Do they have children?
- Is there an income level demographic?
- Are they conservative or liberal?
- What do they read, watch, or enjoy doing?
- What are their hopes, fears, dreams, and pain points?
- Why do they want surgery?

Take your time on this, explore their persona as deeply as possible, and write it all out because you will be using this information later.

Step #3: Write Out Frequently Asked Questions (FAQs)

Write down around 20 questions and answers that address common problems or inquiries given to you by your typical patient profile relating to the particular procedure that you will be writing on.

I imagine this should be really easy for you, as I imagine you are answering these sorts of questions every single day.

Step #4: Identify The Core Problems Of Your Prospective Patient

Now, in order for your target patient to feel like that you understand their mindset and understand their fears and desires, you need to know what their core problems are so you can address that in your book.

There are many ways to go about doing this, and I've listed 5 of my favourite strategies you can use here.

1. Look at the previous questions asked of you from your own patient interactions. What are the top three things patients are concerned about when it comes to a particular procedure?

2. Use online searching facilities to see how people are using your "money keywords" – the keywords related to the main procedure you are writing about – in their online searches.

   You can use Google suggestions (Google suggests additional complimentary or related wording when you start typing into their search bar). It sometimes feels like Google is reading your mind with how accurate these suggestions are! That's mainly because their suggestions are based on the most popular keywords people are searching for.

   Or Quora, where you can use your money keywords again to understand more about how people are using those keywords in current relevant searches.

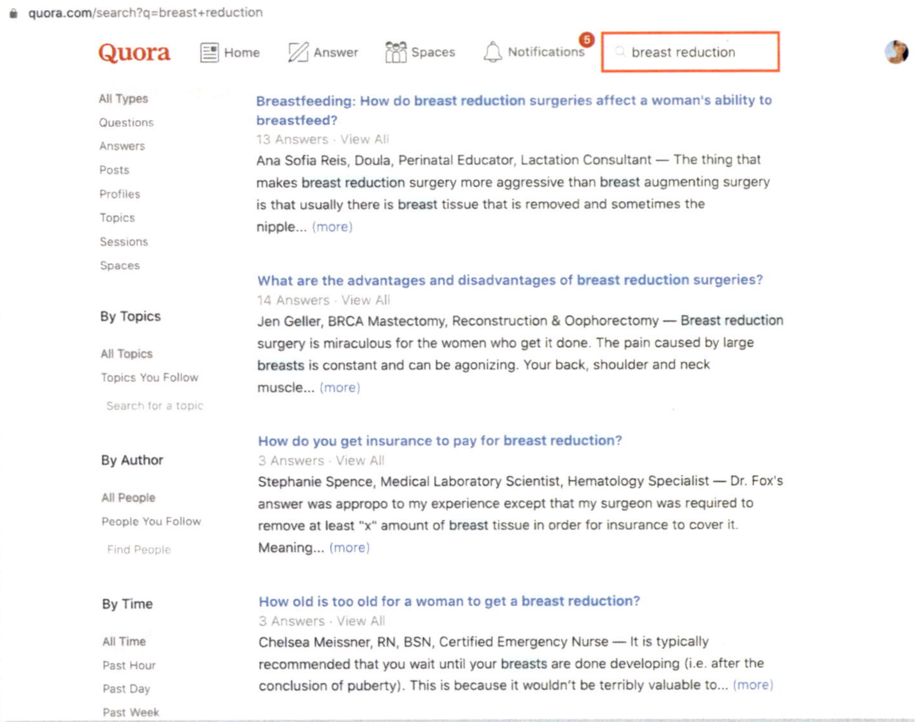

Figure 3: Using Quora.com to see the common questions people ask about a procedure

3. Go to answerthepublic.com and type in your topic and/or keywords and you will see a list of popular questions related to your topic that are being used online.

Figure 4: www.answerthepublic.com has all the FAQs people have used searching for answers online, which is a great tool for developing the content you should be answering in your book.

4. Go to the public forum sites in your niche where your prospective patients like to hang out and find the most popular topics appearing in those forums. For example, specific industries like cosmetic and plastic surgery have;

   www.cosmeticjourney.com/forum/

   www.realself.com/

5. Go to Amazon and find other books that talk about your topic. Sort the books by the ones with the most reviews, look through the reviews to see what people are saying; reading both the 5-star and 1-star reviews. Pay attention to the book titles as well, as that's how they can attract readers first off.

Now, you don't have to do all of these, but it's a great start for understanding more about your prospective patients, and you'll have some ideas about what questions are going through their minds.

And we are done Step #4 already… we are moving quickly! Now it's time to craft an enticing title for your book that speaks to those questions.

Step #5: Craft An Irresistible Book Title

Advertising legend David Ogilvy once said, "On average, five times as many people read the headline as read the body copy. When you have written your headline, you have spent eighty cents out of your dollar".

If you Google "how to create great headlines", you will find a lot of interesting tips and advice, and I'm sure some of them would be applicable to the content that you may want to produce. But to save you time, I've built a simple proven formula to help you craft a winning title for your content, that I have also produced in podcast form, that you can listen to here[1].

1 www.onlinemarketingfordoctors.com/podcast/30/

But to keep it simple for this book, it has been a long-standing belief of mine that writers need to create titles that sell in order to persuade people to check out your content.

It's no secret that headlines and titles have the power to increase your Click-Through Rate[2] on book search results. If your title is boring, people won't click on it. If your title is mesmerizing and captivating, you know that more people are going to click on it.

Your title is **your first best shot** that you have at instantly communicating value, and that same rule applies to your book.

So, let's do a quick test here. These are two books that I found when typing in "breast augmentation surgery book" on Amazon. My question for you is: which book would you click on?

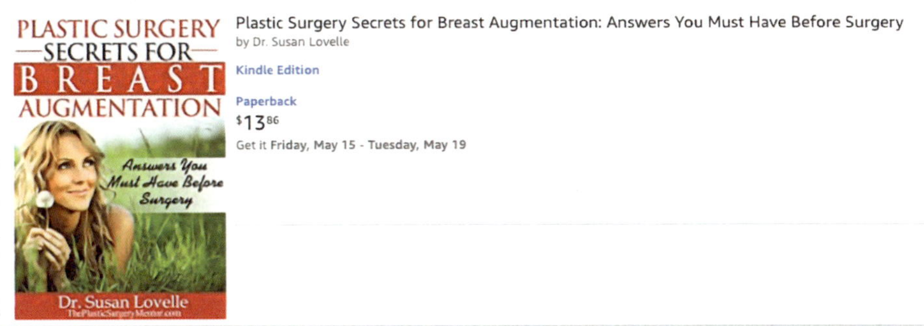

2 www.neilpatel.com/blog/how-to-maximize-your-search-click-through-rate-in-9-simple-steps/

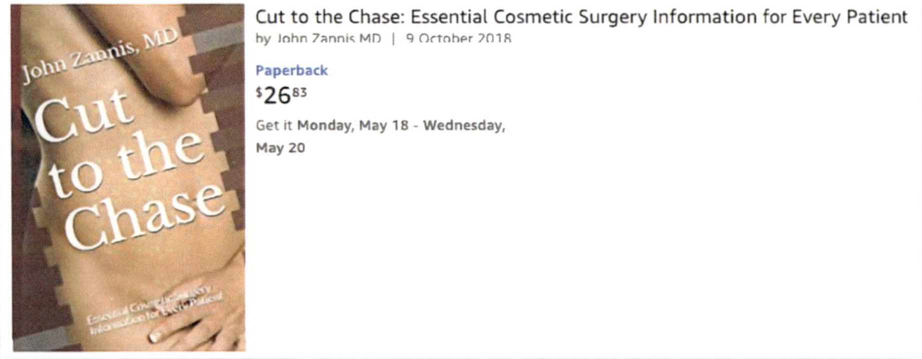

Although I prefer the cover design of the second book, I'll check the first book out first because of the book's title, which is more specific and relevant to what I am looking for. The second book sounds vague and doesn't seem to tell me anything about breast augmentation.

Do you agree?

You need to be crystal clear with your attention-grabbing book title—what exactly will your book say, and what does it address?

You have about two seconds to impress your potential book-buying prospect, and it will be either a "yes" or "no" as to whether or not they will be checking out your book.

Once you have your exciting focus driven headline-grabbing title in place, you are ready to start structuring and writing your book.

Step #6: Outline Your Book

Jot down the key problems and the FAQs that your typical profile patients have (these are the 20 questions or statements that you identified in Step #3 of the process above), and outline bullet-point answers to them on some index cards. Write down each question (or objection or challenge), that relates to your main idea on its own index card, including your response.

Now write three prompt words on the back of each card: these are to remind you how to answer the question that you have posted on the front.

Read through what you have, and pick your favourite six out of the twenty face-down index cards. You will now have your six chapters that will form the basis of what you are going to write.

Order them as logically as possible from one through to six, and you have plotted out the structure of your book.

Step #7: Start Fleshing Out The Details

Don't put those index cards away yet!

You'll need four extra index cards for each of your six chapters. Each of the four cards will have a subheading for the chapter, which will make up your chapter sections.

Here's an example:

- Chapter: How do I choose a liposuction surgeon?
- Subheading #1: Are they registered with the relevant plastic surgeon societies?
- Subheading #2: Do they operate in accredited facilities?
- Subheading #3: What types of liposuction techniques do they use?
- Subheading #4: Do they work as a specialist at major teaching hospitals?

Repeat this for your six selected chapters, using your expertise and experience to answer each of these subheading questions.

Step #8: Introduce Yourself

Now for the fun part… let's get started writing! Don't worry—you'll only need to write a few pages, and I'll explain why in a moment.

But first… your book needs an introduction, where you briefly cover the enquiries your reader may have about you and the content of the book. This doesn't have to be long, just one page will do.

Introduce yourself and your qualifications. Tell your readers about your accolades and what makes you an expert. Then briefly tell your story (remember this isn't going to be all about you, but it helps for the reader to get to know you a little bit first and warm up to you and the idea that you are an expert on this topic).

Tell them why you got into cosmetic surgery. Why did you choose to specialise in this procedure? How are you different from the competition? Most importantly, who is this book for?

Step #9: Record Yourself

Ahhhhh… this isn't so hard now is it? This step is where you can really save your time.

Remember those index cards? You're going to record your answers to those questions you wrote on the index cards. I prefer the amazing RODE Rec or the SpeakWrite app (speakwrite.com). Both are free services, you can choose what works best for you.

Don't worry about making mistakes as you speak. Answer the questions as thoroughly and as best as you can. The "ums" and any grammatical errors will be cleaned up later.

That's the heavy work. You're almost there!

Step #10: Wrap Things Up

But first, it's time to do a little bit more writing again. You only need to write a page, and there's a formula you can follow for ensuring the best result.

Give a brief recap of what you covered in your book. Remind the reader that they can feel confident and ready to take their next steps. This is also where you will include a call to action in the form of encouraging your reader to book a consultation, going to the website, calling the office, etc.

Only two steps left to go, and know that everything else related to the book can be done by other people. That's it for you and writing!

Easy wasn't it? Told ya.

Step #11: Get It In Writing

Pay for a transcribing service to turn the audio recordings you made in Step #9 into text. This is likely to cost no more than $1.25 per minute on Rev.com, and, if you use SpeakWrite's excellent transcription service to turn your audio into text—it just costs 1 cent a word!

Step #12: Sit Back And Let Someone Else Finish Your Work

Once you receive the transcript in a written document format, you need to find yourself an editor who will tidy it all up for you.

If you can find an editor or experienced book writer who can help you with this task, it will make a world of difference, as they will help you write your book in a storytelling format that is more engaging for your audience than just a book with a list of FAQs.

An experienced editor will know how to write it in the same language that your prospective patients would use and connect with them through it.

Online services such as Freelancer (www.freelancer.com) or Upwork (www.upwork.com) can help you hire a professional editor. You can also use these services to find someone to format the book for printing and help with online publishing (if you want) like Kindle and Ingramspark.

The editor will take the completed text file, your introduction, and ending, and they will put it all together so that it reads well and is in a logical order.

And there you have it! A well-written book crammed with useful information just waiting to be published. It should come in at about 80–100 pages, so this is no lightweight tome but a heavyweight contender.

Stop the clock!

It has taken you personally no more than five hours to do this. So, what are we waiting for?

Let's get your book published!

Getting the Cover Designed

The cover's purpose is to get the reader interested in the content of the book. It's just as important as the title. For internet browsing purposes this means that the thumbnail image needs to be clear and enticing.

I recommend to my clients that they search for designers on Upwork (www.upwork.com) or Fiverr (www.fiverr.com) to get the best value for artwork and save time. These websites put you in touch with professional freelancers who can do great work for an amazing value.

However, make sure you're searching for someone who will do a "book cover design" rather than a "3D eBook". Make it clear to the designer that the cover is intended for a printed book. Even better if they have done book cover design before.

You'll need to communicate your requirements clearly. The title and strapline (also known as a tagline) needs to stand out on the cover. This is more important than the graphics, background pattern or anything else.

Ideally, you will get an initial design returned to you within a couple of days, depending on your contract with your designer, and then you can get the printing process started.

You're one step away from getting your book into the hands of readers, gaining that CAE factor, and securing your entry into the elite league.

The Power of Audiobooks

Audiobooks are immersive, educational, instructional and entertaining, and they're perfect for the time-rich and the time-poor.

You can reach and engage a new and different audience through audiobooks through your voice, as not all book lovers like to read. Many people who are dyslexic or just plain busy are buying audiobooks at an increasing rate.

When you are close to their ears, you are closer to their heads and hearts, which can create an invisible connection between them and you even before they see you in person.

Plus, you can boost your print and ebook conversions by adding audio versions so you can reach a wider audience.

By using the methods mentioned earlier to record yourself narrating your book you will have already created an audiobook that your prospects can listen to in their cars on their way to work. If your editor has made a lot of changes, you can consider re-recording the audio files again to get a different version, but I will leave that decision with you.

All it needs now is a little editing and you have another powerful marketing tool waiting to be used.

Not everyone will take the time to read a book, but we can all grab a few moments here and there to listen to one.

Get your audiobook out there and let the patients start coming in.

Getting Your Book Printed

I recommend Amazon KDP (www.kdp.amazon.com) and IngramSpark (www.ingramspark.com) for the actual printing and publishing.

They are both print-on-demand publishers. Using print-on-demand means that you don't need to fill your garage with physical copies of your books waiting to be sold, and when you make a sale, you don't have to wrap and ship the book. Amazon KDP and IngramSpark take care of all of this.

In terms of printing costs, your author copies will cost you anything from about $3.00 to $5.00 for each black-and-white paperback book you print (depending on the number of pages) excluding shipping costs. You can order as few as 1 copy at a time.

Additionally, Amazon KDP will list your print book and Kindle book on all Amazon stores and IngramSpark will distribute your print book and ebook to all other online stores worldwide. I found it quick and easy.

You will need IngramSpark to distribute your book to other brick-and-mortar bookstores as well.

You've got all of the pieces of the puzzle. Now just create your accounts and log in. Amazon KDP and IngramSpark guide you step-by-step through the process.

How exciting is this? You're an established expert. You're now a published author. How many of your competitors can say that?

Now that you've got your book published… what are the next steps?

- Share your book with prospective patients!
- To become the top choice for referring doctors, share your book with doctors!
- If you're going to become the cosmetic or plastic surgeon expert that the media is going to turn to, share your book with the media!
- Keep copies of your book in your waiting room. Share your book with consults and increase your conversion rate!
- Give your book away to capture prospective patients' contact information. More on that later.
- Share photos of you and your book on your website. Improve your Google Ads conversions. It's all about that CAE factor.
- And there are even more ways (endless, really), which I'll outline as we dive into the other secrets of patient generation in this book.

Just don't forget…ask them for positive reviews! There are some book review plugins that you can ask your website developer to add to your book offer landing page, so your existing patients can come in and leave positive reviews for your book.

These reviews can then be used for advertising later on Facebook, Instagram, and Google; which will help you generate more book sign-ups, more authority, and more qualified leads.

I've seen the incredulous looks on many of my client's faces when I've suggested to them that they should be writing a book. I imagine you could be wearing one right now. But for those brave enough, bold enough, and willing to push that little bit extra hard enough; I have seen the results every single time.

What I've given you is only a brief outline, but the tools are there for you to create something informative, unique, and beautiful. This is something that you can do, and can do today! Creating a stellar book that people actually want to read isn't difficult and it will deliver results.

Celebrity status, authority, and expertise are yours for the taking.

You will leave everyone else behind.

Getting Your Book into the Hands of Your Prospective Patients

"If you build it, they will come." That line may have worked for Kevin Costner's character in *Field of Dreams,* but such advice can prove disastrous for your book promotion campaign.

There are still far too many surgeons believing that you can simply build it and they will come as if a clinical practice just magically markets itself.

Marketing is the number one skill you should have when promoting your clinic and your services. This applies to your book as well. Creating a book is one thing, getting your book into the hands of your prospects is just as important.

You are going to need to work hard at getting your new book into the hands of your prospective patients. Here are some quick tips to make it easier on you; and I'll provide more channels and techniques in Secret #5.

Using Magazines and the Local Newspaper

Remember when we profiled your ideal patient? One thing you thought about is what they liked to read; what kind of magazines they flicked through and what newspapers they used.

The reason I wanted you to think about what your ideal patient likes to read is so that you can create a one-page printed flyer detailing a free book giveaway that you can include in that publication. It's also known as a free-standing insert, and it's a powerful marketing tool. It's also a little-used marketing tool in the cosmetic surgery industry, giving you a powerful opportunity to stand out from your competitors.

A free-standing insert is exactly what it sounds like. It sits inside a newspaper or magazine and falls out freely when you give it a flip or a shake. You can use them;

- In your local newspaper
- As a flyer delivered around town
- As the basis of a full-page magazine ad
- Mailed in an envelope

No matter how you use it, if you've profiled your target patient correctly, it will give you great exposure to an enticing offer. Win. Win.

Use Facebook Advertising

I have devoted a whole chapter to Facebook advertising later in this book for the simple reason that it is the fastest way to get your message to anyone that you desire. And it costs next to nothing.

Your book is central to this game-changing strategy, so don't forget to include it in your promotional activities. If you are tempted to skip ahead to check out my detailed breakdown of how to use Facebook Ads, it is in Secret #5. Don't worry… I'll be here when you get back. But don't forget to come back, because otherwise, you'll be missing more great ideas like…

Use Forum Advertising Opportunities

Online forums are places for patients to share experiences and recommendations regarding surgeons and medical practitioners. It's also a place where there may be criticism of people in your clinic, so someone on your team should be checking these forums periodically to make sure there isn't a shockingly bad review out there.

People who hang out in these forums are in the final stages of their decision-making process, they're just looking for some final information before booking a consultation with a trusted source.

Most forums offer some form of advertising option for outside businesses. You can often get competitive rates for banner ads, and all you have to do is negotiate a price.

Get a banner designed (remembering that you can do these sorts of things quickly and cost-effectively from freelance websites like www.fiverr.com or www.upwork.com). A banner ad is just what you think it is: a wide, banner-length image that's used on websites to display or advertise. Think of them as the digital version of a poster or billboard.

Use a banner ad on these forum sites to advertise your free book, making the banner link to the landing page of your website where you offer your book.

Hire an Email Database

Remember our Dream 100 list exercise where we identified what blogs or magazines your ideal patient profile would most likely subscribe to? This now comes in handy for the promotional efforts of your new book.

One of the easiest ways to quickly increase traffic to your book sales funnel is to buy ads in email lists. And which email lists? These are the email lists of the tribes that you've identified from your Dream 100 list.

When I'm looking for email lists to buy space in, I'm traditionally looking for an independent content creator; someone who has already created their own brand and list, where I can pay them to send out an email that highlights and draws attention to my book. The benefit is that it can be a very simple process to ask them if they are willing to sell ad or editorial space in their newsletter, or even my own dedicated email, known as solo ads. The creators who have already had experience with this will typically say yes, and already have some sort of base pricing in place.

You can also find a lot of advertising opportunities in email newsletters by searching on Google. I often type in "[my niche] email advertising" or "[my niche] online media kit", and I can usually find publishers that will sell me a place in their email lists.

I always join their lists for a few weeks before I buy any ad spaces, so I can see how they treat their email list. If they only send a lot of promotional content, then I figure they beat up their list pretty badly and they're probably not the type of list that I want to rent in to.

However, if they send out the good stuff and have a good relationship with their list, then I'll contact them for a media kit.

One thought; independent content creators will often try to sell you "sponsorship ads", which are smaller ads embedded inside their emails. I'm not a huge fan of these, and I've had a really hard time getting them to be profitable. For me, if I can't buy a solo ad, meaning the entire email is my message, then I usually won't do it.

I wish I could give you a set pricing guideline that you'll typically pay, but it almost always ends up as negotiation, as it depends on the size of the list, quality of the list, and the extent of your engagement. Publishers will usually try to have you pay based on how many people they have on their email list because that larger number serves them. But I prefer to pay based on how many clicks their emails typically get.

I'll usually ask to see a report of the last 5-10 emails that they've sent out, and how many clicks each email got. Then what I suggest you do is to reverse engineer the process to determine how much money an ad is worth to you, by asking yourself, if you were to get that many clicks, then based on your current landing page's conversion rate, you should expect to get X number of engagements. And then, understanding how well you convert people into paying clients, you should be able to calculate your Return On Investment and what your ad spend is worth to you.

This process helps me to approximate how much I'm willing to spend to pay for that ad, and I try to negotiate toward that number. For example, you pay approximately $1000 to send an email to a database of, say, 2000 qualified contacts. If 500 people open your email and 10% of those reach out to you, depending on how well you convert them, this could be money well spent.

If you approach it in the right way, you're not going to come across as a spammer. That's the last thing you want. A free book offer as an example would set you apart from those "spammy" emails, because you're offering a free, educational, high-quality book, not a cut-price procedure or product. Interested individuals will respond more enthusiastically to the generous well-intentioned offer, and want to learn more.

SECRET #2: NURTURE YOUR EXISTING DATABASE AND GROW YOUR LISTS

I have been helping cosmetic and plastic surgery clinics skyrocket their qualified lead lists for many years. It's what I do.

With recent changes from Google continuing to push organic search results further down its search results page, Google Ads are still the key driver of traffic and leads for our clients.

One thing that I've noticed, is that for every 100 leads that are generated through your spending on ads; on average, five or less will convert into patients.

But what happened to the other 95 leads that you paid to acquire?

These people might be in the researching or saving money stage, and they are not ready to commit to a procedure as of yet.

Let's be more practical—even with five booked surgeries, I imagine you probably have already achieved a decent Return On Investment.

But as I keep telling my clients, "Your fortune is in the follow-up!". The true value of your investment probably lies in developing those 95 leads that you have gained, and not in resting on those first five patients.

In order to increase your new patient conversion rate, you need to have a proven sales process in place at your practice. That's why I've dedicated a whole chapter on establishing an effective sales process later in this book in Secret #6. Your clinic must nurture these prospects if your leads are going to actually grow.

Consider this; a study showed that 80% of "bookings" are made somewhere between the fifth and the twelfth point of contact.

Only a few are made in the first.

By nurturing and following up on leads, you have the opportunity to build trust with prospective patients. To make them feel comfortable with you, build a relationship, and hopefully gain a future booking from what would have otherwise appeared to be wasted ad spending.

To do this effectively, you must have a clear effective sales process in place. If you think having your practice manager make a phone call when they get a lead, and then scheduling a follow-up call in a few weeks after that is good enough; you're missing out on a wealth of potential growth opportunities.

Let's look at what you need to do to nurture your leads and turn them into future patient bookings.

The first thing you need to prepare yourself for is that you'll want to keep the engagement with these leads in many different ways. One form of media is not enough, because people process and respond to all types of communication differently.

Some prefer visual communication, some respond better to hearing your voice, and others are more engaged with the printed word. So, when you are collecting contact information from your lead, make sure you're collecting the means of delivering these different forms of communication.

Your sales follow-up process should include all of the multi-modality means available to you for following-up. Follow-ups can be sent separately or combined together, but they should include;

- Automated SMS
- Follow-up phone calls
- Personalised emails
- Printed letters
- Voice Drops
- Remarketing Facebook Ads

If users are not converting from the initial follow-up campaign, move these users into a maintenance list where you are sending out automated newsletters on a regular basis (twice a month) about useful tips, advice, the latest research, treatments, technology, and updates about your clinic and its doctors.

This ongoing engagement will ensure that you will be at the forefront of their mind when they are ready to enquire about your services. And this relatively small amount of work will make a huge difference in the number of leads that you see converting into patients.

Here are a few ways you can start communicating more effectively in your follow-up process and make your ad spend continue to work for you, long after that click has generated a lead.

Set-Up an Email/SMS Auto-responder

Email and SMS marketing software is critical when it comes to marketing and sales.

If prospective patients sign up for an initial consultation or any other irresistible offer that you have available (like your new book!), auto-responding software can be used to remind people about their next steps in the process, which can be anything from booking the time for that first consultation or just providing additional useful information about the procedure.

Not only good for keeping you front of mind with any prospective lead, but this software will free up your administrative staff from having to manually follow-up personally, and provide an opportunity to create a continuous level of engagement with your prospects, while your staff can focus on other lead converting activities.

I love automation, and my team and I have helped many practices automate their communications process to help them save time and money.

If you don't have any email marketing software up and running at your practice, we recommend any of the following options;

- Go High Level (email, SMS, Facebook Messenger, WhatsApp, Viber...)
- Mailchimp (email marketing software)

- Keap (email and SMS marketing add-ons)
- Drip (email and SMS marketing add-ons)
- ClickSend (for SMS marketing)

Using your new book as an example, a follow-up sequence would begin with 5 separate emails, and these communications would be sent over the course of 20 days as people may be taking the time to go through your book.

For those who don't become your patients or are not ready for advancing your engagement further after this period, you can move them into a "Maintenance" list where you should be sending them newsletters/emails twice a month.

We also recommend that you supplement those 5 emails with additional follow-up communications, using any of the additional forms of follow-up we discussed earlier;

- SMS
- Phone calls
- A Letter (old school!)
- Voice Drops

These additional forms of communication are meant to supplement the foundations that you are laying out with your email sequence. These added communications could be simple reminders to look out for your next email or to confirm that your lead has received a previous email. Or for more advanced communications; it could include follow-up information or added details in regards to your email content, that you mentioned that you will be sending along separately.

Want a real example? Let's take your book as an example, and imagine a scenario where you've made it available for free on your website for people who give you some contact details.

If you're not sure what you should say in each of those follow-up email communications… no worries… I've got your complete email plan here.

Below, we've outlined the 5 specific emails that you want to send out during this period, and what should be contained in each. The remaining components, like SMS text messages or phone calls, you can add in as you feel necessary.

Email #1 (Sent out immediately)

As soon as a lead requests your book by submitting their online form, you want to let them know that you're the taking action type. You want to send off a confirmation email follow-up to them immediately.

You will need to write the content of that email specifically, but the contents should contain;

1. An acknowledgment that their request was successfully completed and registered.
2. Congratulate them on their wisdom for making the decision to get your book.
3. Provide contact information, such as an email address, should they have any questions.
4. Reinforce the benefits of the book to build their anticipation of receiving it.

5. Mention the link for them to leave a review of the book once they have read it.

The key here, of course, is that the book is shipped immediately too. Let's not delay!

Email #2 (Sent 2 to 5 days after the book was shipped)

The second communication in this follow-up series should be sent out after the book has been shipped and you are reasonably confident the book could be in their hands. Depending on how the book is shipped to their location, the timings for this could vary, so it wouldn't hurt to give a buffer day or two just in case.

Optimally, this second communication should land no more than two to five days after the package has arrived, and it needs to include the following;

1. Congratulate them again for getting the book.
2. Lay out the benefits the book offers, what they will learn, and the transformations that someone can achieve from the procedures detailed in the book.
3. Reinforce the need to go through the book completely, if they haven't done so already.
4. Introduce your procedure and any special offer that you may have in relation to the procedure for those who have gotten the book. (Such as a free consultation if booked within the next 15 days of getting this 2nd email)
5. Provide a final strong call to action; such as, pick up the phone or email me to find out more.

Email #3 (Sent 10 days after the book was shipped)

In this email, you want to start developing a more personal relationship with the lead and start further adding to the impression that you are the celebrity authority in your industry.

You can accomplish this by writing an email for the lead that contains a relevant story or case study that is representative of your typical profiled patient. Try to include details of how the procedure addressed key pain points, and provide some great before and after examples or videos.

Add a few reviews from third-party websites to further help boost your credibility, and a final call-to-action to book in an initial consultation, or to give your practice a call for more details.

Email #4 (Sent 15 days after the book was shipped)

At this point, it is likely that your prospective lead might be holding back, doubtful on either the procedure, the benefits it could give them, or other personal considerations. At this point though, it is safe to assume that there are some doubts.

To address these supposed doubts, we want to use this 4th email to amplify the amount of information that they have access to, that might be able to address those silent concerns that they might have.

Use this email to focus on frequently asked questions, (bonus points if you decide to make your email content include a video of you), or talk about a recent interview or professional presentation that you gave about the same procedure. If you have a webinar or a video series about this procedure, you can invite them to join and watch that too.

Whichever path you choose, the goal here is to provide more valuable relevant content and be the answer to their questions.

Email #5 (Sent 20 days after the book was shipped)

The final communication in this series of emails should ideally go out around five days after the previous 4th email. As this will be the last communication you'll have in regards to the book, and trying to use it to gain a lead, you'll be using this last email to provide closure on your follow-up process.

The email should be written to accomplish the following goals;

1. Confirm that by now they've had time to read and appreciate your book.
2. Describe why you can be trusted to deliver on your promises.
3. Reiterate any special offers you have in place in regards to the procedure discussed.
4. Close on a firm final call to action once more.

Your series of correspondences may have ended here, but your relationship with your prospective patient is not over yet; regardless of whether they respond or not. Today's database contacts are your patients of tomorrow.

By adding them to your "Maintenance" lists after they've exited this follow-up process, ensures that you develop a continuous ongoing engagement with this lead, which will hopefully end up with more business down the road.

Important Notes About Email

Using email effectively in your follow-up process is an art and a science. First, it is the most common form of communication that marketers use to engage, so it is hard to cut through the rest of the marketing noise online. You need to up your email game.

Most people are overloaded with emails on a daily basis, and so we shouldn't be surprised when we don't get a response from any of our emails.

As challenging as it may be, regular quality communication is a must, and so we must find the best strategies to make the most of our email communications. After all, it builds trust, offers ongoing opportunities to take the next step and keeps you front of mind.

In general, be consistent by sending out a newsletter/email to the people in your database every single month. For some reason, others in this industry are just not doing that. But by sending out a regular monthly newsletter/email will give your practice a huge advantage, as there is a good argument for maintaining regular contact over the long term.

I myself once bought a Facebook ads online course from an author after 6 years of being on her email list. She won me over in the end, after all those years, following up with great content and convincing me that she had the information I valued.

Remember, that success doesn't come from what you do occasionally, it comes from what you do CONSISTENTLY.

It's likely that a lead has been in touch with more than one practice. It's also likely these other practices aren't consistently maintaining contact with that lead. It's their loss and your gain.

When your lead is finally ready to go ahead with a procedure, it's probable that your practice will be the only practice that has remained in regular contact with them. At that point, who do you think they will choose to be their service provider?

How to Write the Perfect Email

For effective use of email, keep your emails short and sweet. They should be direct and to the point, and not demand too much attention or commitment from your prospect. They should be engaging. Witty, light and entertaining. Personal and value-added.

Seems easy right?

Okay, so writing great email content might not be everyone's cup of tea, so I've simplified it for you, and highlighted three key tips that you'll want to follow for getting yourself closer to writing the perfect email. If you are interested, I did a whole podcast on this topic, that outlines more useful and insightful tips that can help you write better emails.

Those tips can be found in our podcast #47[3]. But these three are the most important for getting people to see, open, and engage with your email content.

1. Use a killer subject line

Everyone has an email inbox that is being constantly filled with work requests, newsletters, and junk mail; and the one thing that keeps us from hitting the delete button on any of those emails is the subject line. So, improve your email success rate by crafting a killer subject line for your emails.

---

3 www.onlinemarketingfordoctors.com/podcast/47/

There are a few things to remember when writing a subject line.

- **Spark curiosity**: It should entice the reader to open your email and want to read more. Make it fun and relevant to your email content.
- **Keep it simple**: Your subject line shouldn't be more than 50 characters. Ideally no more than five words.
- **Be descriptive**: Sometimes it's best to be direct but not repetitive.
- **Don't over-promise**: Clickbait tactics, which trick patients into opening your email, might work the first time but it won't have lasting effects long term.

Do you know what was the subject line for the most opened email in history?

"Hey"

Who sent it?

Former President Barack Obama.

No, really. It was casual, straightforward, and unexpected from one of the most powerful people in the world. So that explains a huge part of its success. I mean, how often do you see an email from the President of the United States that just says "Hey"?

But the better question to ask is, "Who wouldn't open it?"

That unusual email played a role in his re-election, but it wasn't the only one. Other catchy subject lines included "Join me for dinner", "It's officially over", "It doesn't have to be this way", or an equally simple, "Wow".

They're all personal, and they all relied on curiosity and intrigue to get the user to open the email.

You may not be Barack Obama, but you can write equally curiosity inspiring subject lines.

2. Talk to them like a friend

So, how do you cut through, get noticed, and eventually sell to your lead?

First…don't try to sell them straight out of the gate. The focus should be on getting your message read. To do that, an email needs to be personal. Writing in a friendly tone is a good way to start. It's perfectly fine to start an email with "Hey there". Let people get to know you a little bit. Be quirky.

Many companies use their emails to just sell, sell, sell; and their writing reflects that. Using short sentences and writing the way you naturally speak makes for good email copy. Make it approachable.

The last thing you want is an overwhelming wall of text when someone opens your email. Write in small paragraphs or single lines of copy for information that's easy to consume.

When it comes down to it, nobody likes being sold to. They want to hear from their friends. Your task is to sound like a trusted friend or colleague *without* being gimmicky.

If you don't get it right, you'll lose trust and those emails will never see the light of day. You'll see poor email metrics and even worse—email blindness, where people tune out from your emails as quickly as they see them.

3. Strip out your graphics

While your email subject line is one of the primary ways to get an email *opened*, the design of your email is how you get it *read*.

You might think that a beautifully designed email containing a lot of images, animated buttons and an HTML-enhanced responsive theme would increase the number of people that will read your emails and click through on your desired call-to-actions, but this couldn't be further from the truth.

Contrary to popular advice from seasoned marketers, your email shouldn't look "beautiful", with heavy images and sexy graphics.

Why not?

Who do you think sends these types of heavy emails with a lot of images? Is it individuals or businesses with commercial intent? Of course, it is businesses!

People see email as a personal one-to-one form of communication, and when was the last time you got a beautifully designed HTML-enhanced email from a friend about something important?

Simple plain text emails better reflect the personal nature of email, while HTML-enhanced emails scream "commercial mass marketing", and are easy to delete.

Ideas For Email Content

As I mentioned previously, if a lead doesn't go ahead with your services after going through an initial follow-up campaign, you should put them into your "Maintenance" sequence, where you will be sending them emails twice a month to keep in touch.

The importance of frequent newsletters is beyond doubt, but it somewhat begs the question of what information should your practice include in these fortnightly missives? Generating ideas for newsletters can seem daunting, and so we've provided a list of content ideas that you can use for your future newsletters.

Please keep in mind my three tips for writing these emails that I just outlined. It is applicable for any communication between you and your leads. And as always; keep your emails personal, engaging and value-added.

12 Newsletter Content Ideas

1. **A Patient's Journey**

   A patient telling their story is extremely powerful and can be used as a testimonial for your practice.

2. **Great Before-and-After Examples**

   If you have recently captured some great before-and-after results, be sure to share them with your list. You can make it more visually engaging by using "Before and After Slider" apps on your phone to create short videos with your pictures. (SlideApps, Before and After Pro Slider, Diff Before and After Video are just a few of these apps)

3. **Employee Spotlight**

   Put a human touch on your clinic by highlighting some of the outstanding staff at your practice.

4. **Practice News and Events**

   Have you participated in an event recently? Spoken at a conference? Participated in a charity event? Spotlight these stories in your next newsletter.

5. **Editorials**

   These think pieces address your thoughts on a particular subject. If your specialty is breast augmentation, you may want to discuss your impressions around using fat transfer to breasts. These editorials will further establish your expertise and inform prospective patients.

6. **Blog, Video, Podcast Excerpts**

   If you publish awesome podcasts, videos, or blog content, extend their life by sharing excerpts of them in your newsletters.

7. **Media Mentions**

   This could be a one-off guest article featured on another website, an interview on a TV show, or regular videos, podcasts, or blog articles you publish, either way, you can highlight these media mentions in your newsletter to build more credibility.

8. **Special Offers**

   If you have special offers, then a newsletter is a really great place to raise more awareness of that. You can even time the announcement of the offer so that your database is given priority treatment.

9. Q&A

    If one person is asking, it is likely that many more people are wondering the same question. Answer frequently asked questions in your newsletter. This can be a one-off article or as part of a regular feature.

10. New Service Announcements

    Introduce a new staff member or a new service that you're offering at the practice. Let prospective patients know about the launch of a new product or service first, to make them feel special about being one of the "first to know".

11. An Event Calendar

    If you appear at conferences or expos, tell your database about these dates to draw awareness and maybe increase attendance. It further builds up your CAE factor.

12. Case Studies or White Papers

    These are in-depth looks at the latest research. It's another way to help establish your authority and expertise.

The Power of Text SMS

When it comes to useful means of communication, it isn't just email anymore. Have you noticed that texting is everywhere? Just look around. You won't have to look far to see that people are constantly checking and responding to their text messages.

Meanwhile, phone calls are on the decline. In fact, studies have shown that people see incoming phone calls as an intrusion in their lives. Many people don't even answer incoming phone calls, and if you think it's fine to just leave a message, you might be surprised to learn that 19% of people[4] never check their voicemail. Ever!

One key positive aspect of using text messages for your communications is that currently, **marketing text messages is by far less crowded than email,** as people are not getting hundreds and hundreds of text-based marketing messages on a daily basis.

The fishing is best where the fewest people go, and not many people are willing to text communicate with leads yet, so this allows for you a better chance of success at getting your communications read.

When using a text message as part of your follow-up process, it's important to treat it in the same way that you would when you're texting a friend. Don't cut and paste a big email and send it as a text message. Text messages should be a short one- or a two-line bit of personal communication.

4 www.openmarket.com/press/study-millennials-would-rather-text-than-talk-infographic/

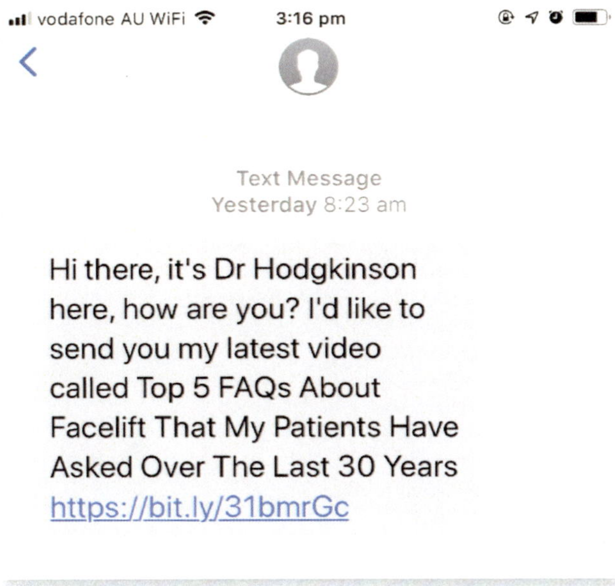

Figure 5: Example of valuable, friendly SMS content

The purpose of sending a text message is to help engagement and to provide more value to the receiver; you can send a quick video of a procedure, a link to one of your case studies, before and after images that are similar to their case, or even a great review.

Whatever you are adding to the message, just remember that it should be done with the intent of adding real value to that process.

SECRET #3: BUILDING YOUR ONLINE REPUTATION WITH INDEPENDENT REVIEWS

If you've come this far, I know that you've determined the niche that you want to dominate, you've written a book and leveraged your mailing lists for generating an ongoing flow of new patient enquiries.

Our next secret for building your celebrity authority in your chosen niche is to get this audience of current and previous patients working for you. You need to get them to build your online reputation by writing positive reviews about you, your services and your practice.

Any positive review is extremely beneficial to your reputation. But if you want to dominate your niche, you need to generate more positive reviews than your competitors are.

Let me ask you a few simple questions;

- Do you know what your patients are saying about you online?
- Do you have a strong five-star reputation?
- Are you personally responding to negative reviews?
- Do you have a strategy to gain more five-star reviews?

Prospective patients can be incredibly thorough when researching for a surgeon. After all, surgery is a big undertaking! One of the very first things many of them will do is Google "your name + reviews".

If you haven't done this already yourself… you should. Now is the time to see what people have been saying about you online. What you find, can make or break your ability to gain new patients.

All of those advertising dollars could be going to waste if someone wants to find reviews of your services online, and they come across something like this...

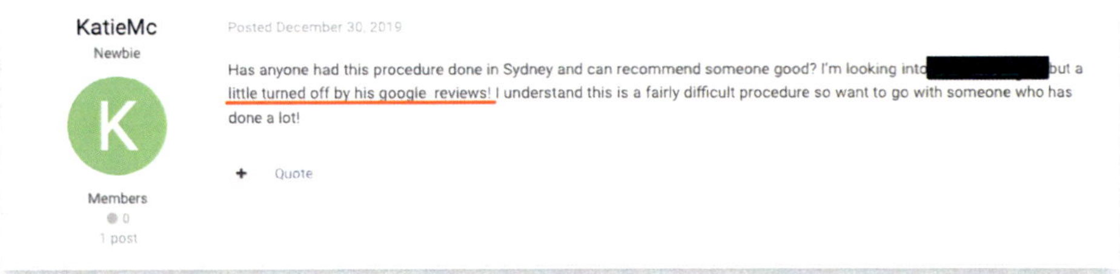

If your prospective patients can't find you, or even worse, if all they see are negative reviews or just a few non-descript reviews when they are searching you out online, they will most likely just move on to the next surgeon that they are thinking of going to see for a consultation.

So, the question is… how do you build your online reputation?

First, we need a spot where we want to direct your patients to leave their reviews. My recommendation is to turn to these 3rd party review platform websites for the medical profession;

1. www.google.com/mybusiness/ (International)
2. www.realself.com/ (United Kingdom, Australia)

3. www.ratemds.com/ (International)

4. www.realpatientratings.com/ (United States)

5. www.cosmeticjourney.com/ (Australia)

6. www.plasticsurgeryhub.com.au/ (Australia)

7. www.healthengine.com.au/ (Australia)

I recommend these websites because typically they will appear first when someone searches for your name looking for reviews. But you can also consider other local directories in your area that allow post-op patients the opportunity to review your services honestly in a search engine-approved testimonial format.

There are also many other online forums, chat groups, and social media networks for patients to share their stories and recommend surgeons to other members. These areas also have a frequency towards criticising surgeons, which is why you should have someone on your team monitoring these areas for bad reviews.

The reason testimonials on 3rd party sites are credible and can help influence your standing is that they are independent. People can be upfront and honest about their experiences. Genuine online testimonials are the digital equivalent of a positive word of mouth referral.

Which is better than an anonymous testimonial on your practice's website that someone could think was fabricated or that could have been posted by anyone.

Remember your potential patients aren't necessarily going to look at the most immediate spots for help or answers, they are savvier than that. They will be looking for clear independent non-influenced feedback for establishing concrete proof that they can trust you.

I could write a whole book just on reputation management. It is a very broad, and quickly evolving space. But fundamentally the challenge is the same for everyone; "How do I get more online testimonials?".

Simply put, you will get more by encouraging and empowering your patients to write reviews about their experiences with you on independent forums, like the ones I listed earlier. Let's break down the best means available to you;

1. **Ask them in person**

   If a patient seems happy with their results following your services, you need to feel comfortable with asking that patient for a review. It may feel taboo, but most people are accustomed to being asked; everyone is asking for a review these days, from Uber to their supermarket.

   Emphasize that this will mean a lot for you personally, and you'd be appreciative of them writing a review for you. Too many surgeons won't ask, and you need to move past that if that includes you, especially if you really want to lift your credibility and your practice.

2. **Have it done at your office**

   While the patient is waiting for you in the waiting room for a follow-up meeting, that is a great time to ask them to write you an independent review. This could be done through the help of the practice manager, or even by leaving an iPad or computer setup in the space. Make it as easy as possible for your patient.

3. **Postcards**

   If you aren't comfortable with having to directly ask for a review in options 1 or 2, hand out thank you cards requesting a review and listing the sites where they can be left on.

4. **Emails**

   And finally, as part of any post-operative care emails that you send, make sure you directly ask for a review. Please also keep in mind to follow up as well.

As I said before, the fortune is made in the follow-up. And patients who have stuck with you, and kept supporting you beyond their immediate needs, are much more likely to leave a review—and a positive one at that.

Getting reviews isn't easy; *you'll need to work just as hard for reviews as you do to deliver your services.* Make the process clear and easy for your patients, and don't be shy with asking. Your online reputation is too critical to your success to leave to chance, and changes won't happen overnight.

But by getting started today, establishing a process and laying the foundation for a consistent process of encouraging more reviews, you'll start seeing exponential growth in your patient numbers as your reviews continue to promote you and your services on your behalf.

"Good marketing makes the company look smart, great marketing makes the customer feel smart."

JOE CHERNOW

SECRET #4:
USE CONTENT TO DOMINATE SEARCH AND SOCIAL PLATFORMS

Content Is King

If you want to be at the top of your niche, you have to establish yourself as the go-to person for that category in terms of content.

Why?

Because content is king.

Through content, you can make your prospective patients feel smarter by educating them and giving them all of the content that they could possibly need or find about your niche.

You might be thinking, *"Whoa… Huyen, I've already published a book, isn't it enough?"*.

The book was just a great foundational starting point to build your celebrity status. You need to continuously produce new and valued content to keep up your celebrity authority status and to continuously stay ahead of your competition.

Nobody got labelled as the GOAT (Greatest Of All Time) in their respective industry by just stopping after their first taste of success.

Instead…they continuously worked hard on their game or making new hits or in a surgeon's case – staying informed and educated on the trends, challenges and opportunities in your industry.

Your job as the celebrity authority is to do the same. In order to maintain and grow your celebrity authority status, you have to keep pushing forward.

In this 4th secret, I'm going to outline exactly what you need to do to produce more "hits" and how to get thousands of people following you and your content online, so you can completely dominate all social and search channels, leaving your competition in the dust.

Value-Based Marketing – The Marketing Choice For Plastic and Cosmetic Surgeons

One early morning years ago, as part of my morning ritual, I started reading some marketing articles online and came across a webinar talking about value-based marketing, and how it started in 1948.

Value-based marketing is based on the simple premise of "giving before asking". People are 10 times more likely to come to you to learn something than they are to be sold something. *It* is an appeal to a prospective patient's *values* and ethics. It shifts *marketing* from a practice-centric approach to a patient-centric one.

Marketing is often seen as "showing off". Telling people how great you are or what you can do for them, and making claims about the results someone can achieve if they go through a procedure with you.

But these days, prospective patients simply don't believe that message. It isn't a unique message. Every service provider in your space is driving home a similar message. And more importantly, none of that proves to a potential patient that you will be able to deliver the results and value that they're looking for.

What does prove you can deliver that value they are looking for is by *demonstrating* it, rather than *claiming* it. Show them that you can help them by *actually* helping them as part of your marketing effort. How do you do this… by leading with value.

For high-valued cosmetic surgery services, at least 80% of your leads won't be ready to buy when they first contact you.

Maybe you meet them at an event and they're interested in your presentation. Or they've come to your website and downloaded your free book, or watched an insightful video of yours. Or maybe they attended a webinar you hosted.

In most cases, that first contact is more about reaching out to gather more information, not a desire to become an immediate buyer.

So, you need to provide more than that, for you to turn that lead into a client.

Instead, you need multiple value-adding interactions. You need to build credibility and trust in specific areas for them to feel ready to buy. And you need to be top of mind when the time is right for them.

This is why value-based marketing is my recommended marketing choice for cosmetic and plastic surgeons who sell high-valued procedures.

A few decades ago, a journalist named Lewis from Jacksonville in the United States, placed the first-ever value-based ad in a small regional newspaper for the financial investment company Merrill Lynch.

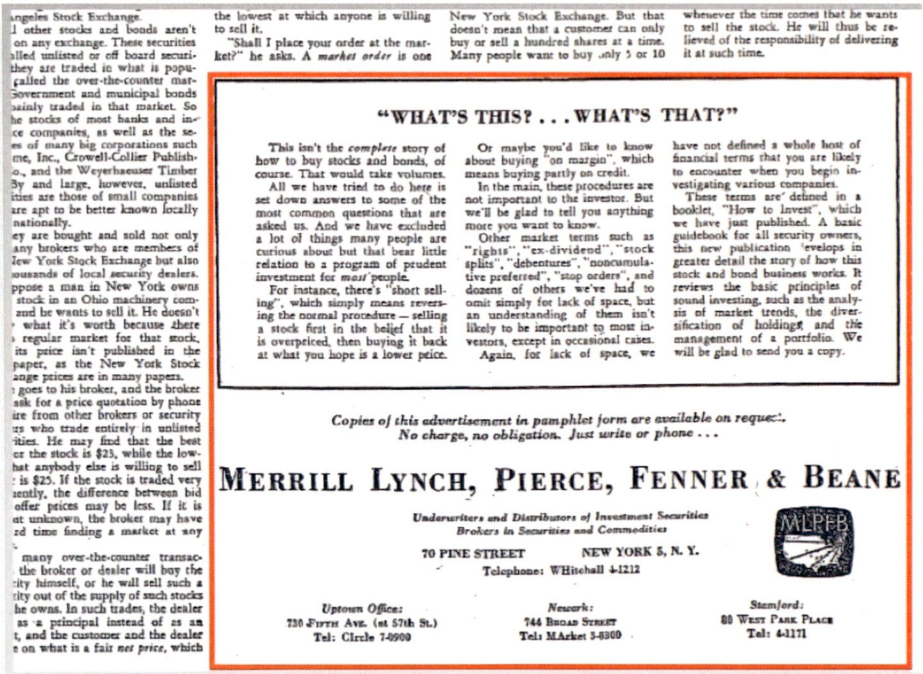

Figure 6: The first successful value-based ad in the world, by Merrill Lynch, featuring a guidebook called "How to Invest", which was offered as a freebie to public investors

The ad campaign was so successful that in its first week of running, the ads pulled in around 5,000 leads. And in the 1950s, they didn't have easy online registration and contact web forms like we have today. This is 5,000 people actually physically cutting out a piece of paper and filling out the form and mailing it back to Merrill Lynch. That is how adding value can gain you more leads.

The greatest ad man in the world—David Ogilvy—later decided to model and perfect this value-based marketing concept. He went on and created 17 ads to sell his own ad agency's services, and those 17 ads helped Ogilvy & Mather sell more than $1.4 billion worth of ad revenue in the 1970s.

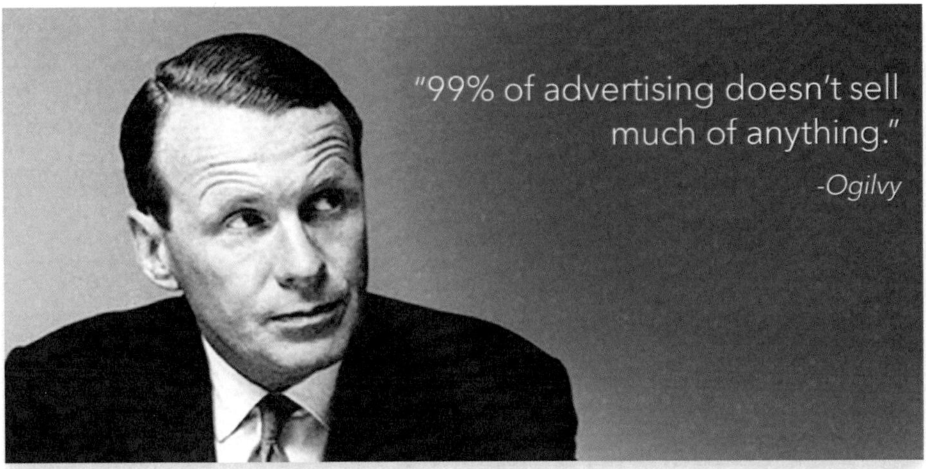

I have been a strong advocate for more value-based marketing initiatives ever since I was first introduced to the concept that one early morning years ago. I think it perfectly suits professionals, especially doctors and surgeons who don't want to come across as sleazy or salesy in their marketing approach.

When you produce content that gives value to your prospects and educates them, you don't need to sell them. Instead, you will be building trust with them, and eventually, they will come to you.

Type Of Content To Produce

When it comes to value-based marketing initiatives, there are many different types of content that you can produce, including;

- Webinars
- Videos
- Case Studies

- Livestreams
- Podcasts
- Blog Posts
- Reports
- Whitepapers
- Images

People resonate differently to various types of content, but if you are looking to start somewhere, I would suggest starting with moving images first. Any content with visuals and sound will be more engaging than static content: video, webinar, podcast, etc… but if I had to pick just one; my answer is a simple video with captions.

Why captions? Because up to 85% of Facebook video is now watched without sound[5]. We can't expect that everyone who ends up seeing our videos, will be watching it with sound.

I recommend video because I appreciate that you are time-poor, so you need something that you can create quickly, that generates the highest impact. Video can do that, and much more. According to Cisco, video will represent 80% of all internet traffic in 2020.

Over half of all video content is viewed on mobile, and 92% of mobile video viewers share videos with others. People are 10 times more likely to share good video content compared to other photos and blog posts. In short, video is very powerful.

Plus, you can easily convert or embed video content into other types of content, including;

5 www.digiday.com/media/silent-world-facebook-video/

- Podcasts
- Video blog posts (with transcripts so you can rank on organic search results!)
- Videos used in a newsletter and automated email follow-ups campaign
- Social media (Facebook, Instagram, YouTube, LinkedIn, etc.)
- Google My Business listing posts

With just one piece of video content, you can use it on many different platforms, and with many different purposes.

Video is taking over the mobile digital marketing landscape, and video content will be the key driver of a mobile-first marketing strategy this year and onwards.

Are you worried that you won't be able to create great video content? Don't worry. I will show you how to create great videos in no time with only a smartphone, and an easy online tool for adding captions cheaply, in the "Make Your Life Easier" bonus section of this book.

How Often Should I Produce Content?

Creating content is one thing, but promoting it is equally important. No use creating great content if it just sits in the folders on your computer. I'll show you how to dominate your online channels with your value-based content in the 5th secret next.

You should be committing to producing as much content as you can support through your promotional activities. Your content is the bridge to getting to your target audience. It's the trust-building tool that we use in this online world. That's why I would prefer quality content over quantity.

I suggest creating at least two videos a month. If you can produce more... and support it... please do! You will never suffer from having access to great value-based content.

What Content Topics Should I Choose?

The process of finding content topics is pretty similar to what I outlined in the "How To Publish Your Book" section.

You should always start with your patient's FAQs and the latest news/ research about the procedures that your target audience cares most about.

When you get stuck, you can always check out this amazing tool, www.answerthepuplic.com; that takes your keywords and gives you the most asked questions and popular search topics online relating to those keywords.

Figure 7: A comprehensive list of "liposuction" online queries and searches generated by the answerthepublic.com tool

Real Examples of Unique & Effective Content

I'd like to show you how other successful plastic surgeons completely dominate their category with their creative content in different formats.

Creating a Social Community

Dr Kourosh Tavakoli's nickname is the "King of Boobs", and he obviously knows his target audience very well: women in their 20s who love to show off their bodies on Instagram.

You may have heard of Victoria's Secret's Angels; the top-tier lingerie models who are considered some of the most attractive women on this planet. Dr Tavakoli[6] followed this concept and cleverly created a community of his target audience who want to self-nominate themselves as an "angel" by posting sexy post-operative images. He encourages his patients to show his work, and build his community, by using his #DrTavAngel hashtag on Instagram.

Figure 8: Example of using the hashtag #DrTavAngel in user-generated content

Dr Tavakoli is a great example of a surgeon using many of the strategies that I've outlined in this book. He knows his target audience's desires, frustrations, needs, and wants…thoroughly. That's why he has been successful with his marketing. It is clearly focused, and the messaging stays consistent with the niche he is trying to grow.

6 www.instagram.com/drtavakoli/

Figure 9: Merchandise that features "Dr Tav Angel" to further promote the brand

He's established himself as the king of his niche; breast augmentation. While he still performs other procedures, his outbound content and the message that he is promoting is very consistent with that "King of Boobs" persona.

And this outward messaging doesn't stop with his previous patient's Instagram posts. He embodies and showcases a personal lifestyle that demonstrates a closeness to his ideal target patient's desired lifestyle.

Figure 10: Dr Tavakoli wearing a Gucci shirt, flying in a private jet on his holiday; imagery that would resonate with his target audience's dreams

If you want to see more, I would highly encourage you to check out his Dr Tav TV channel[7], to see more of the types of content that he produces. They are varied; from presentations and demonstrations to informative and fun. And while they look great, they rarely would require much effort to replicate. For example, the video slideshows of a patient's before and after images can be done well using the video creation apps that we discussed previously.

Educational Video Funnel

And of course, you are now asking... *"Well, that looks easy enough, but what if your target audience is not a twenty-something woman,*

7 www.youtube.com/user/DrKouroshTavakoli

but rather a middle-aged woman who doesn't aspire to such grand promotions of oneself on social media?".

Of course, the images and content that is being pushed out by Dr Tavakoli isn't going to resonate with that audience. But that doesn't mean that there isn't an effective strategy for cornering that target audience.

Faced with a similar target audience, the world-renowned surgeon Dr Darryl Hodgkinson positioned himself as an expert facial surgeon; looking to dominate the market with his signature facelift. And instead of using quick flashy social media content to reach his audience, he used educational videos to create a video funnel that captured his target prospects attention through an irresistible headline and special offer.

Figure 11: Dr Hodgkinson attracts his target audience using educational, mobile-friendly content

Another great example of an educational video series is from Dr Gavin Chan[8], who is known for his honest opinions about dermal filler and anti-wrinkle injections. He has created a massive number of followers on YouTube and other social media channels, with thousands of comments on each of his videos.

8 www.youtube.com/viccosmeticinstitute

Next Level Video Content - Webinars

For those procedures that prospective patients generally need more information and education on (which is most of them) before proceeding with, a webinar is an effective way to educate, engage, and establish trust and authority with them.

There isn't a marketing channel or tool that can address the 3 key elements of a buying decision—the Know, Like, Trust elements — in a 40-minute window like a webinar can.

With webinars, you can pre-record them; so you can easily put your best presentation on autopilot online, ready for attendees to join at any time. Webinars are a great scalable way for you to generate serious leads, without requiring additional hours of phone and in-person consultations on your part.

Of course, making a webinar sounds daunting, but it doesn't have to be. There are many people creating high-quality professional webinars every day, using nothing more than their own laptops to do it.

There are also online tutorials and courses that will show you an easy step-by-step process that you can follow to create an Automated Webinar Sales Funnel[9] of your own. I'll talk about that in more detail in the "Make Your Life Easier" bonus section of this book.

9 www.onlinemarketingfordoctors.com/webinar-sales-funnel-course/

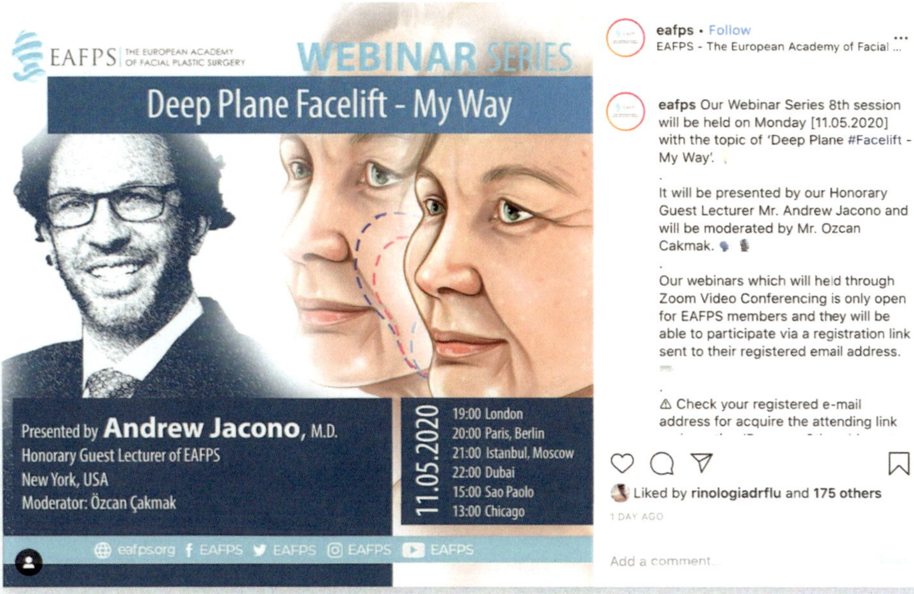

Figure 12: A webinar series about your niche is a great way to educate and generate serious prospective patients

"Marketing is no longer about the stuff that you make, but the stories that you tell."

SETH GODIN

Other Content Types

As I mentioned before, there are many different types of content that you can produce, and while video is my preferred favourite, there are a couple of other content types that can produce incredible results for those using them effectively.

Patient Stories

People become connected and engaged with the stories and characters that are described in our stories. Using previous patient stories is an effective way to show your prospective patients more about how you've seen the challenges that they may be facing previously.

You know and have seen, the struggles both physically and mentally that someone in their position may be experiencing. And you get to show the relatable journey that your previous patient committed themselves to and achieved, by having a procedure done, which changed their future positively.

These shared stories, and shared journeys, are very powerful ways of motivating and influencing decision making.

Figure 13: A patient story done by Me Clinic

The rise of the Instagram one-minute video, Facebook Live, and Snapchat shows us that telling a good story isn't limited to long-form engagement. Many people have found creative ways to demonstrate their stories in these shorter accessible formats. You should consider adding them to your marketing mix too.

TV Show

And finally, if you have a decent enough marketing budget, and a good relationship with a media producer, this is an undeniably great way for you to gain media exposure and generate celebrity level attention with your prospective patients.

Figure 14: The Cosmetic Surgery Show, featuring Dr Daniel Lanzer.

"The best marketing doesn't feel like marketing."

TOM FISHBURNE

SECRET #5: SIMPLIFY YOUR MARKETING EFFORTS

Your opportunities for marketing have never been easier, cheaper and more varied. It has also never been more confusing, challenging, and when done poorly, a significant waste of time and money.

But if you are going to dominate your niche, your presence needs to be equally dominant in these marketing opportunities available to you, or else you'll be losing valuable presence to your competitors.

And so, where to begin? With so many options, which avenues should you be targeting?

Before starting this chapter, I want to give you a high-level picture of what you need to do in order to dominate your category with search engines and social channels.

When working with a marketing agency, you need to brief them on your positioning and target audience and ask them to make sure that you are present where your target audience is hanging out.

It should start with the website and other digital channels that you are on and make any required changes to reflect your clear positioning as an expert in your chosen niche.

*Figure 15: If you want to position yourself as a facial surgeon, then your website copy needs to reflect it clearly. This is an example of positioning Dr Hodgkinson as **the** choice, not just **a** choice, in facial cosmetic surgery. Once you know how to position yourself as **the** choice, patients will find that it is easier to connect and commit to you.*

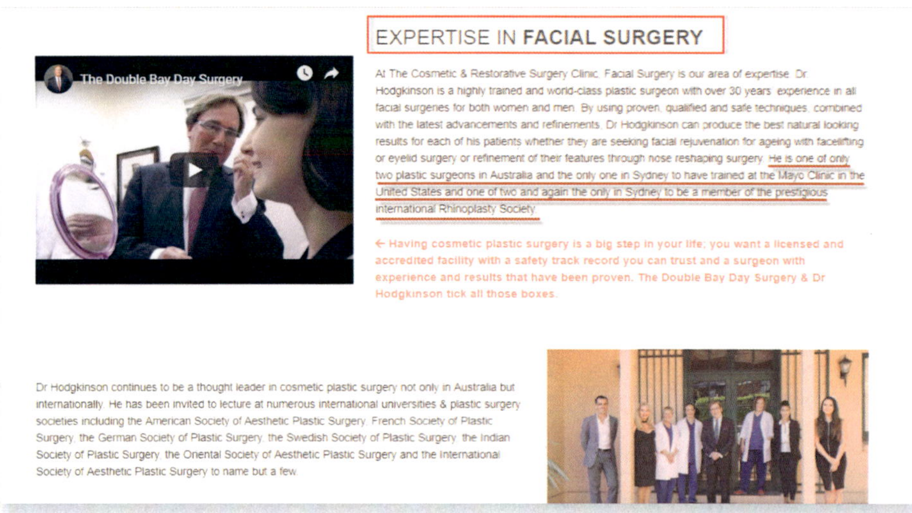

Figure 16: Highlighting the unique expertise qualities that supports your position as an expert

Then when it comes to search engines, whenever people type in your niche keywords, you need to show up high on rankings.

For example, if you want to dominate the "liposuction" niche, then when it comes to liposuction-related keywords, you should be at the top results for both organic and paid ad listings.

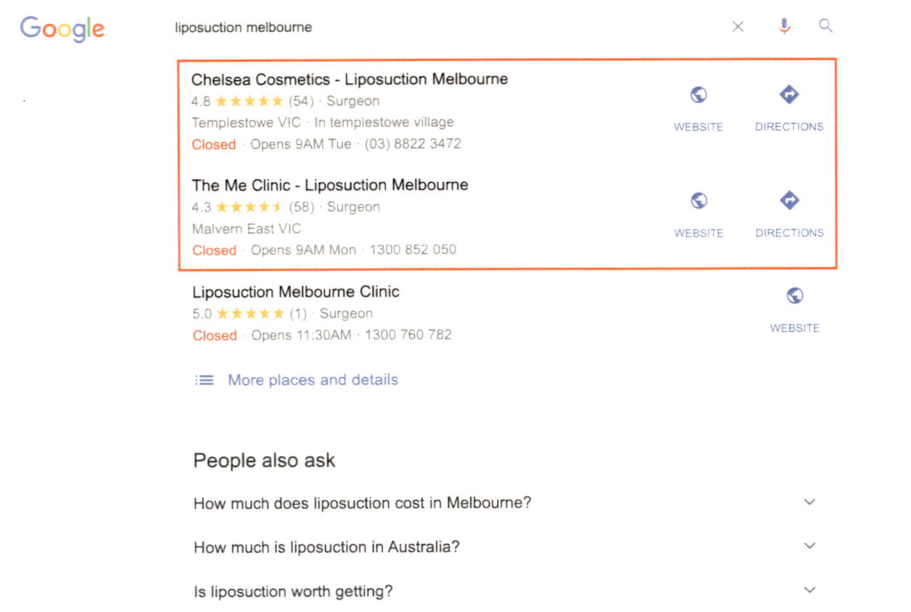

Figure 17: Chelsea Cosmetics and Me Clinic are leaders in liposuction, therefore they are ranking on top of local Google maps

When it comes to social media channels (Facebook, Instagram, YouTube, etc.), your content should be pushed out to your target audience, including your book.

In order to reach your audience more effectively, you should use search and social media ads, and while I'm going to walk you through the different channels you could use to promote your new book, you can apply these same techniques for any other piece of content that you produce.

Things To Keep In Mind When It Comes to Advertising

1. You Don't Need To Be Everywhere

The desire to get your advertising anywhere and everywhere is strong. And that may be the right strategy, or it may be the wrong one for you. The key to knowing what is right for you and your practice is understanding where your targeted profile patient is hanging out.

Most people are engaging with some level of social media in their lives; Facebook, Instagram, Linkedin, Snapchat, Tik Tok... the list is getting longer and more complex by the day. But focusing your efforts on the platforms that are being used by your targeted profile patient, will help you save money, drive better conversions, and lead to more success.

2. Ad Strategy Should Be Built To Retain The Attention of Cold Prospects

Because cold prospects will represent the largest segment of your search market, it is key that your ad strategy is built for retaining their attention beyond them simply seeing your advertising.

Targeting these prospective patients is ultimately where the biggest potential lies long-term. But to warm them up, you'll need to develop a clever sales funnel approach to your marketing, utilizing education-based content, like promoting the book that we developed earlier in Secret #1, to draw people into a slow-developing nurturing relationship.

What do I mean by sales funnel?

A sales funnel is a process that you build; a journey that you take your typical ideal patient on, from when they first engage with one of your ads, until they emerge out the bottom of your sales funnel ready to be a client.

All funnels are different in length and content, but the process of each is the same… start by offering an irresistible special offer (let's say your new book!) in exchange for their contact information.

Then you can send periodic messages through those communication channels building a story/narrative around your services, offerings and yourself as a desirable service provider until they become so impressed or interested, they are calling you looking to be a client.

While you could manually manage this process, the best sales funnels are built automatically and use the same software that we discussed earlier to nurture your database in Secret #2. But all sales funnels begin with advertising to a cold audience, offering to trade that valuable content of yours, for their contact information.

Where should you start advertising your special valuable content offer? Again, wherever your targeted profile patient is. But in most cases, that will be Google and Facebook.

Their numbers are so big, and their ability to target specific groups is incredible, so you can really get laser-focused with your targeting. Getting your presence on these platforms will be invaluable to your practice, and your perception as the celebrity in your chosen niche.

3. Prospecting Ads vs Retargeting Ads

Before I talk about ads, I need to take a minute to explain the difference between "prospecting" ads vs "retargeting" ads.

Prospecting ads is the act of reaching out into a network to find cold traffic or people who aren't familiar with you and hook them long enough to get their attention. After we've gotten their attention and gotten them to engage with us (engage could mean that they have watched, liked, or commented on an ad), then we move them from the "prospecting" pool into a "retargeting" bucket.

We then advertise to these retargeting people differently, and work to warm them up with different ads (or stories) and remind them of the great offer you had that initially got them into your sales funnel process; which using our book as an example, would be: Book Sign Up – Initial Consultation – Surgery Booking.

4. Targeting For Prospecting Ads

The next step after you have made ads highlighting your special offer is to figure out who to show it to.

Dream 100: The best place to start is with your Dream 100 list, which we discussed earlier in this book, for that platform. When you're running ads on Facebook and Instagram, you can target people who have an interest in a certain thought leader, brand, or celebrity. You'll find many (but probably not all) of your Dream 100's followers targetable this way in Facebook's Ads Manager. For YouTube, you can specify that you'd like your ads to show in front of your Dream 100's videos both individually or their channel as a whole.

Ideal Patient Avatar: Second on your targeting list is your ideal patient avatar. Think about their interests, age, their career, their home life, and anything else you can identify. Most of these ad platforms will allow you to get pretty specific on who you show your ads to.

Overlapping sections of multiple audiences: Some ad networks let you get more specific in targeting your audiences by layering on multiple criteria and then just targeting overlapping sections.

An example of this would be to not target just Kim Kardashian's followers in one campaign, mothers with kids in another, and women between the ages of 35 to 55 in a third campaign, but instead to have one campaign that requires your prospect to be in all three of those categories in order to be shown your ad. Be smart with your audiences and layering them can really help you focus and narrow in on your target audience, while also bringing your costs down while improving your results.

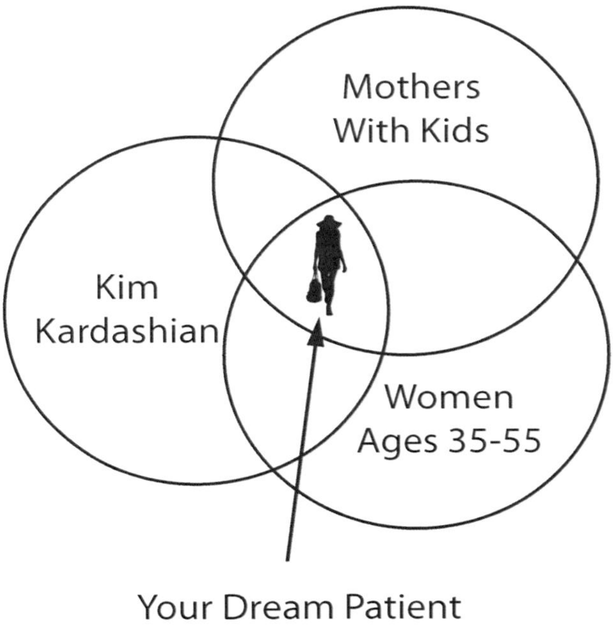

Figure 18: When you target overlapping sections of people, only targeting those who have multiple characteristics in common, you can bring down your ad costs and get better results.

Algorithms: Ad platforms today are getting much smarter, and can work with your targeted patient profile to help you to reach out to other similar lookalike audiences. In Google and YouTube, they're called Similar Audiences, and in Facebook and Instagram, they're called Lookalike Audiences. In both cases, you decide which profile persona you'd like to use as the source, and then the algorithm will look deeper beyond your immediate inputs, and then match up against other people in your specified geographical range who are most similar to that audience, and thus more likely to be interested in what you have to offer.

5. Not All Prospects Are Ready To Buy Right Now

Only 5% of search users are in hot buying mode as they are hunting around the internet. The other 95%; are searching in researching mode, sourcing information, and are a much colder audience.

In Secret #2, we talked about the power of following up with our prospects using follow-up funnels. But what about all of the people who will watch your videos, or come to your funnel, but don't give you their email addresses? How do you follow up with them? The answer is through retargeting ads.

Here's an example to show you how it works.

- Let's say you spend $2,000 on some ads.
- From that, you get 100,000 people to actually see your ads.
- The ad performed well and 4% of those people engaged with the ad (4,000 people).
- And 2% of the original 100,000 clicked on the ad to go to your funnel (2,000 clicks).

- Of these people, 30% of them give you their email address.
- And 10% become prospective patient leads (60 leads)

That leaves 3,940 people who engaged with your ad but didn't become a lead or a buyer. While you'll never be able to capture everyone's attention, you can in fact reach a lot more. How? This is where retargeting comes in.

There are three specific audiences that are essential to a high-performance retargeting plan. Each is based on how far viewers got along the customer journey.

Audience #1 – Engaged: These people interacted with your ads (comment, like, share…) or visited your website but they did not sign up for your offer or enquire about your services.

The goal of retargeting ads is to **Sell The Click**, meaning we will create ads that follow them around the internet, highlighting your special offer, <u>for up to five days</u>, trying to get them back to your special offer signup landing page. If they haven't visited your signup page after five days, you can let them fall out of your target audience group used for retargeting purposes.

Audience #2 – Landed: The second audience you'll want to build is made up of the people who clicked through and landed on your special offer signup landing page, but they didn't sign up. While these people trusted you with their curiosity and visited your signup landing page, they didn't take any further action by opting in for your special offer.

The goal of the ads for this audience is to **Sell The Book Opt-in**. You can run a retargeted ad to this audience for <u>up to seven days</u> trying to get them to come back and take you up on your lead magnet's special offer. Again, if they don't sign up within seven days, you can let them fall out of this remarketing audience.

Audience #3 – Owned: The third type of audience you'll want to have is made up of those who did take your lead magnet offer, but didn't see it through to being a patient. These people have made a large commitment and have entrusted you with their email addresses and phone numbers.

This is the traffic that you now own, and it becomes very useful and lucrative in many different ways. Not only are they now in your follow-up sequences, but they're also prime candidates for seeing ads for your next offer which could be a complimentary or reduced-fee consultation with you. Therefore, the goal of the remarketing ads for this group of audience is to **Sell The Next Step**.

To understand this better, think of people as moving on a certain conveyor belt. While they're on a specific conveyor belt, they're shown the ad that is appropriate to them; you're hoping they take the hook and find themselves in a new audience on the subsequent conveyor belt. If they don't take the hook, they move off that particular belt and find themselves back in your prospecting pool awaiting the next hook that intrigues them.

Of course, you're now probably asking; how can you create these custom audiences and set up different retargeting ads to follow them? I don't want to overwhelm you with all of the technical aspects of it, you just need to understand the overarching strategy, and ask your Facebook marketer to implement it for you.

Please keep in mind that the lowest hanging fruit in the advertising world is running ads to your subscribers, followers, and ever-growing email lists that you own. While only a third of the emails you send may get opened, you can always run ads to your email lists, often reaching those who didn't originally open emails and greatly increasing your overall conversions from these lists.

Your #1 goal is to transition the traffic that you are earning and buying into traffic that you own by taking them through one of your front-end funnels, which in our example could be your book.

What I've outlined here is a very effective strategy that will work on Google, YouTube, Instagram, and Facebook as well as other ad platforms. The technology of these platforms will be constantly changing, however, the strategy behind how to identify your target audience, where they are hanging out and how to get them to see your message will never change.

There are many different tactics and little things you can do to increase your ad's effectiveness, but by following the strategy outlined here, you can always be sure that you're hitting the right people at the right time with the right message.

6. Your Ad Campaign's Job Is To Obtain Clicks

Getting cold audiences to click on your ads is an incredible challenge. And a challenge that I see many advertisers getting wrong all the time.

Typically, when I see clinics using Google or Facebook ads to sell their procedures, they're attempting to use the ad to convince prospective patients that their clinic is the best clinic that a prospective patient would want for their needs.

And that's ridiculous because it rarely works well to sell somebody directly from your ads. Of course, you could catch some fish, but when was the last time you saw a Google or Facebook ad and bought from it directly without even clicking on the ad or checking out their website?

Your ads should demand attention and compel readers to click further, not to buy. The sole purpose of your advertising is to get the attention of your dream buyer as they race by on the information superhighway (I still love that term!).

So, it begs the question—how do you get their attention and what motivates their click?

The answer is a primal desire that can be provoked in several ways;

- Curiosity and intrigue
- Shock
- Direct benefit
- Implied benefit
- Fear
- Vanity
- Self-interest (Better, stronger, faster, healthier, happier, sexier, filter, smarter)

To illustrate this, I conducted a quick Google search on "breast reduction Sydney". You can see the results here…

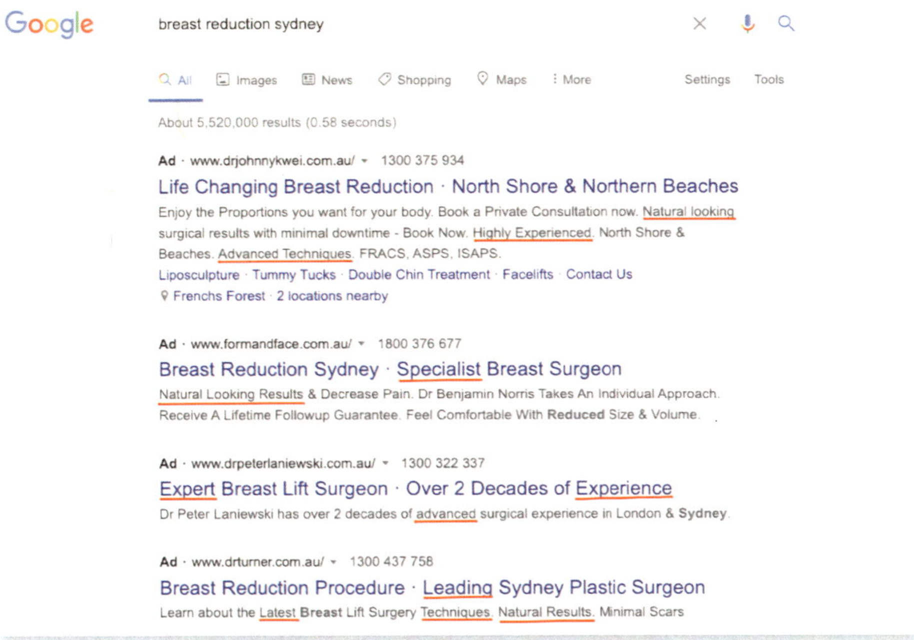

Figure 19: Do you notice that all of these ads look quite similar, and use more or less the same statements?

I've highlighted a few key terms to draw your attention to how these ads all start to look and sound the same. They even all start with the same words "Breast Reduction". None of them stand out or demand the searchers' attention.

What are these ads actually trying to do? Sell me!

Right there in the ad copy, they are trying to convince the searcher that they're the ones who can help me. You should choose me. And now. This is like asking someone to marry you on the first date.

These ads are all using similar wording, including; "Natural Looking Results", "Advanced Techniques", "XX Years Of Experience", "Specialist", "Leading", "Expert", "Highly Experience", "Book Now", etc.

This is such a common approach, and in such a crowded and congested digital space, absolutely the wrong way to approach it. Instead, we must fight to obtain that click, we need to get your ad to stand out so we can get more people to click on your ads.

Simple enough. Let's get to work.

First, we need our ad to sell our valuable content. In this example, I'm going to focus on the presumed book that we wrote in Secret #1.

Next, we assess the environment in which our ad will be competing for attention. We already know all the ads start with "Breast Reduction", so we must do something different here to stand out.

After a little research and using the strategies I outlined in this book, I came up with a fictional title and concept for our book that allowed me to get my creative juices flowing, and I came up with the following ad;

Ad · www.exampledomain.com/Breast-Reduction-Guide-Book ▾
Considering a Breast Reduction? 9 Things You Wish You'd Known
Must-See List of 9 Things Every Woman Considering a Breast Reduction Surgery Should Know.
Patient's True Story Revealed All - Free Book (Published on Amazon), Download Now!
1,230 Downloads – Usually $69 Now FREE – Ends Soon – Act Now – Hardcover & Kindle Version

This simple ad demonstrates the key fundamentals of;

- Dialling up the intrigue with the "9 Things You Wish You'd Known" headline.
- Partnering this with the question "Considering a Breast Reduction?" to initiate a conversation with the searcher, and please Google's need for ad relevancy using keywords used in the Google search.

I then tease what's on the opt-in page, and the benefit to come for clicking on the ad with: "Must-Have List of 9 Things Every Woman Considering a Breast Reduction Surgery Should Know."

Nothing about this ad is selling anything. No one is immediately encouraged to buy anything based off this ad; so what am I trying to sell? I'm offering something that's so irresistible, something that has so much more intrigue that people can't help but click to learn more.

I then go on to build the social proof ("1,230 Downloads"), add urgency ("Ends Soon – Act Now"), and a call to action ("Download Now") to help solidify this ad as a standout option for searchers to click on.

Now let's see how my new ad shapes up in the environment where it has to compete for attention. Which ad are you more likely to click on? Which one stands out? And which one has intrigue oozing out of it?

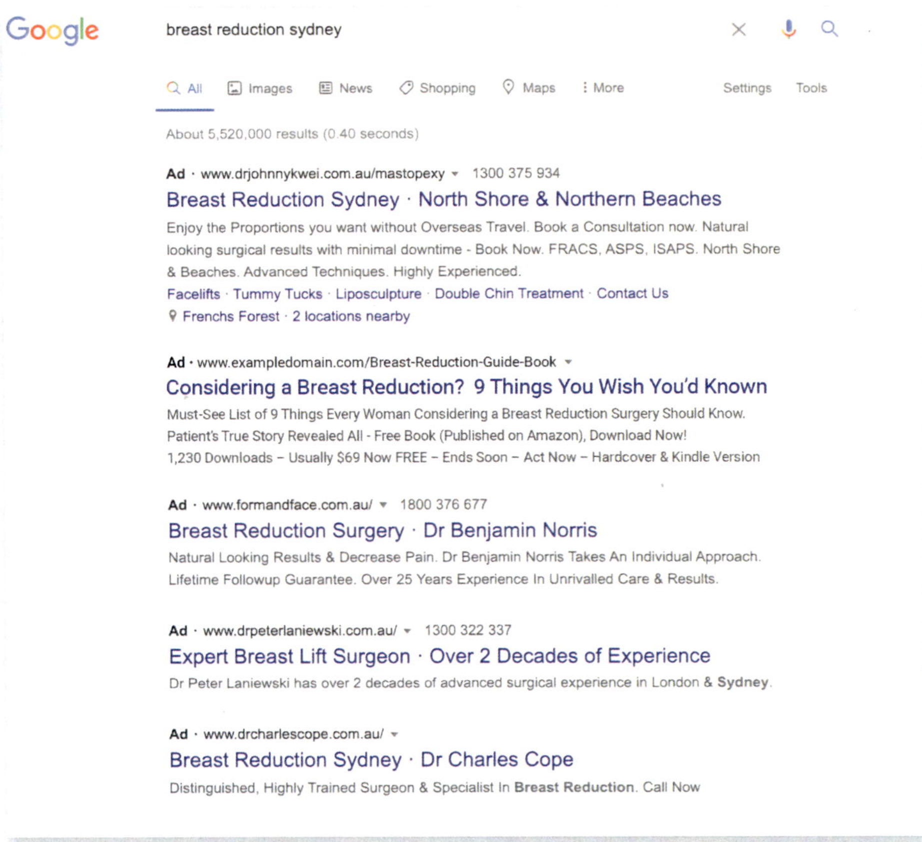

Figure 20: Which ad would you click on?

This is just one simple example. Opportunities like this exist in all cosmetic markets. This one strategic shift can make you stand out from your competition, funnelling the majority of prospective patients into your business.

But your opportunities for promotion aren't limited to just Google ads. You've got a wealth of options available to you. I'm going to show you the best FREE and PAID channels available that you can use to effectively promote your book (or other value-based content), for easily drawing in more patients to your practice.

4 Best FREE Marketing Techniques

1. Email Your Contact List.

I've mentioned this technique earlier, but I'd like to add some points when it comes to marketing to an email list.

The major benefit here is that your contacts already know you, so all of the efforts you are going through to try and build trust with your audience has already been established. And while it is possible that previous patients may not need your specific services anymore, they may have friends and family who do, and they can forward your emails along to them.

Some good tips when sending out an email to your subscribers is to make sure that the email is personalized for each individual member; use their name in the email at minimum (depending on what emailing marketing software you use, the personalization syntax is different; ask your email marketing software provider about this).

Don't forget to include the best-selling points of your special offer in the email, and resend the email to those who didn't open the email the first time around, as they may have missed it. This can be done automatically by your email marketing software.

Pro Tip: Don't forget to mention the special offer (especially if the offer is your book) in your regular newsletter and email signature as well. You should also ask your existing contacts to forward this offer around to someone they know or their additional contacts who might be interested or could benefit from this material.

"If content is king, then conversion is queen."

JOHN MUNSELL

2. Website Promotion

The benefit here is that you are leveraging your website's existing traffic.

For a cosmetic surgery clinic to expect website traffic to generate a good amount of ongoing leads, your website traffic should be getting at least 1,000 visits a month. And, based on my experience, once your website reaches 10,000 visits or more a month, you can expect a healthy stream of prospective patients to your practice.

Having a lot of traffic is one thing, but when 95% of website visitors aren't calling or enquiring immediately, how do we find better means of developing a longer-term engagement and conversation with them?

This is when we use a promotion on your website of your special offer (Get my new book!) to act as a lead magnet, attracting these 95% of website visitors to not just casually surf on by, but to invest in trading their contact information for your special offer. Getting these surfers to opt-in to your special offerings begins that conversation and relationship that will improve your future conversion rate, and it helps to establish trust and authority in you and your services.

The best way to promote a special offer like your new book on your website is by creating an opt-in page or a dedicated landing page for your website visitors.

Unlike a traditional website page, this new dedicated landing page will have only one single clear focused message, which is to get the prospective patient to sign up for your special offer.

This landing page shouldn't have any other call-to-actions or menu items on it to distract prospects who land here from taking the desired action that you want them to do.

Figure 21: Example of an e-book special offer opt-in page, with a clear call-to-action button appearing above the fold

You should also mention your special offer in the website's header and footer or a home page slider. Further, increase your promotion by considering adding a sidebar onto your subpages for greater exposure regardless of which pages your website traffic is on.

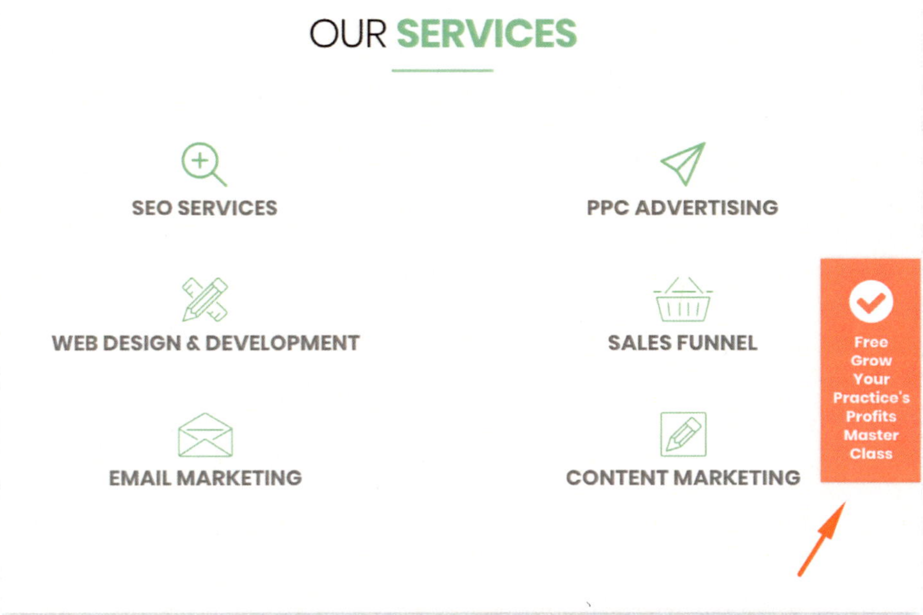

Figure 22: Example of a website sidebar's banner featuring a masterclass

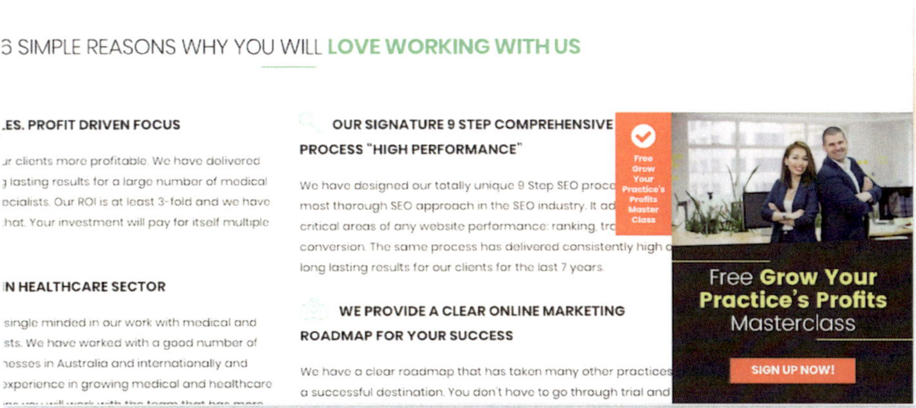

Figure 23: Hovering on the sidebar banner, expands a display of the book image with a clear call-to-action button

And finally, an exit pop-up on your website is another great option for promotion as well as further mentions on any relevant page/blog article throughout the website. You may need to ask your website developer to help with this, it would be a simple task for them to do.

There are many places on your website for building the promotion of your valuable content, helping to drive as much traffic to your special offer as possible. So, don't feel limited to just your website's header/slider.

3. Feature on Your Social Media Channels

You've spent a lot of time building a profile on social media, take advantage of it now by promoting your value-based content special offer through your social media channels by updating your cover photos and making ongoing posts about it.

Facebook, Instagram and YouTube are all great options to consider if you aren't using them already. Facebook and Instagram are especially useful, as they can link directly back to your website's special dedicated landing page that we discussed earlier.

You can use repeated postings over a period of time to keep reminding people too.

If you have the ability or hiring someone who can, animating images for your social media posts is helpful for getting your posts to stand out among a very crowded landscape. The more attention-grabbing your post (the image and copy) can be, the better.

The bonus section in this book mentions some apps that you can use to help you convert single images into fun animated video clips for more engagement.

Pro Tip: Don't forget to snap some behind-the-scenes action photos, as they can be a lot of fun to post on your social media channels to help sell you and your relatability.

Additional Pro Tip: Facebook has a pixel called the custom-audience pixel. This pixel allows you to track the people who visited your website, and if those people are also on Facebook you can actually put all of those website visitors into a special targeted group inside of Facebook for running your ads too.

The Facebook pixel can be a very powerful tool when marketing using Facebook ads, as it can build a typical profile of your audience and can help you find other similar audiences moving forward on your behalf.

And don't forget, you can also create custom audiences for the three different groups of audience that I mentioned earlier in this chapter (Landed, Engaged and Owned), so you can retarget people who have engaged with your ads at different stages, but haven't moved forward with your services yet. Make sure it is installed!

4. Facebook Live and Instagram Stories.

Currently, Facebook Live & Instagram Stories is getting great exposure on social media, as Facebook is actively trying to push this format to the top of its news feeds.

You need to take advantage of this, as many people aren't using this format yet; you can move to the head of the class very quickly, increasing audience interest, building trust and awareness.

If you have not used Facebook Live yet, it is best used by recording yourself facing directly into the camera and being personal and in the moment. Use a fun and engaging headline and copy like, "My first published book is out!"

My final favourite FREE marketing technique is to use Instagram stories. It's similar to Facebook Live except that they are shorter, immediate, and are only available for viewing for a short time period post-recording. They are, however, quickly becoming a preferred method for people to exchange information on Instagram.

It is a common misconception that promotion and ads should be an expensive proposition. And hopefully, I've demonstrated that promotion of your valued-based content doesn't have to be expensive and that you can see some real benefit in using these FREE techniques.

5 Best Paid Marketing Techniques

But, as good as those free techniques are, there are some even more effective paid options that you should be exploring too. The pool of paid marketing opportunities is pretty limitless and some of the techniques that we aren't covering, like radio, print, and television can provide value—any marketing that gets in front of potential audience members has value—but the costs involved limit the overall return on investment and make it difficult for me to recommend.

The basic principle is to go back to the Dream 100 list and identify what are the top channels, platforms, community groups that your target audience are congregating and target those channels.

If you are feeling inspired to generate more promotion via those means once you've completed the 5 techniques I'm going to recommend here, go ahead—I wouldn't discourage it. But to get the best return on your investment, these 5 paid techniques are tops.

1. Use Facebook & Instagram Ads

Despite recent changes to Facebook Ads; how they are used/ displayed in Facebook and the increase in costs, they are still a great way to target your profiled audience. Just a quick note to clarify, Facebook owns Instagram and you can advertise on Instagram using Facebook's Ads platform, simplifying the process for you.

There are many benefits to using Facebook Ads, as Facebook is still the most popular social network and it is very easy to direct your ads to a specific audience.

Some other benefits include the ability to retarget your existing website visitors, email lists, and find a similar audience to those groups, for easily reaching new potential markets.

Here are four simple steps for setting up a Facebook ads campaign.

Choose your target audience

I described earlier in this book, how to determine your target audience.

When creating your book in Secret #1, I asked you to profile your target audience and identify your Dream 100 list of tribes that your target audience is a member of. If you did your homework you are about to reap the rewards because this information is going to come in handy when you choose the people you want to show your ads to on Facebook.

To give you an example: for one of my clients, the most profitable audience has proven to be a female parent, between 30-45 years old, with a child under three years of age, who lives within 30 kilometres of Melbourne. It helps to get very specific. You can have multiple specific profiled groups, but each one should be really nailing the specific details of the majority of people in that group.

Don't forget to retarget your website audience and its similar audience, and use the email addresses from your email list and its similar audience for more detailed targeting.

And finally, target the Facebook pages, groups and people that your target audience is following, your current fans and their friends, as this is a great way to increase the reach of your audience.

Set your budget

Starting cautiously is fine, but allocating at least $20 USD per day is an absolute minimum to ensure your ad gets good exposure within your targeted group.

Write ad copy and select an image/video

With the ad copy:

- Highlight the benefits of your valued content (It's my new FREE book!) to the audience
- Create an image carousel ad to promote it visually
- Use emojis to make your ads pop
- If possible, also create a video of you talking about your valued content and special offer, and why a prospective patient should want it.

Please make sure to record your video in a vertical format and add captions to it, so it can be more user-friendly on Facebook and Instagram. Up to 85% of Facebook video[10] is now watched without sound, so adding captions to your video is essential. I use rev.com as a captioning service, or you can hire a freelance video editor to help you create a professional video with captions.

Figure 24: An example of the Facebook carousel ads I used to promote my book

10 www.digiday.com/media/silent-world-facebook-video/

follow-up process & a lot of practices don't have a proven process in place to make this work.

👉And finally, I'm giving you and your team an actual sales script to follow, so that you have an actual proven strategy for creating an engaging conversation with a potential prospect, and how to deal with the different situations or challenges that they can present.

⬇️Download this guide, have a read, and send it to whoever is in charge of your sales process at your clinic and ask them to follow this process.

🎉I guarantee you'll see the changes immediately after just a few calls.

‼️Get this guide, and improve your new patient conversion rate today!

https://onlinemarketingfordoctors.com/samurai-sales-guide/

ONLINEMARKETINGFORDOCTORS.COM

🔥LAST CHANCE! YOUR $200 DISCOUNT EXPIRES ON MAY 15th 2020

7 FIGURE SAMURAI SWORD SALES GUIDE FOR CLINICS

Get Offer

13

1 share

Figure 25: Use video in your Facebook ads to generate more engagement than using static image ads

Activate your ad campaign

Sit back and watch the leads come flooding in!

Pro tip: The big secret that helps well-known authors in the digital marketing world like Dean Graziosi and Russell Brunson sell around 5,000 copies of their books per week, is that they create many more ads than a normal campaign. They create a few new ads each day. More creative. More hooks. More ads. Now, if you could manage to create several new ads per week, you are in a very good spot already in terms of promoting your book. Your ads will look fresh all the time, with varied and new copy/imagery to keep your audience interested and engaged.

Making new ads doesn't have to be complicated. Carry your book with you all day long, and every time you find a cool spot, you can pull out your phone and make a new video ad. For example; at your kid's basketball game, at your house, at the airport, hiking, going out for dinner…etc.

When you're thinking about making new prospecting ads, you're looking at a huge ocean of people- all who need your service or product but all who have a different reason why. If you try to create just one hook, it may last for a while and grab the people looking for that hook, but it will dry up very fast.

You should be prolific at creating new ads. The phone in your pocket will become your ad-making, creative–generating, hook-developing machine. Everywhere you go, you should be looking for opportunities to record a pitch for your book that you can then turn into ads for Facebook, Instagram and YouTube channels.

Keep in mind that the more ads you can put out, the more success you will have. Use all these hooks to grab your dream patients from prospecting pools, pull them into your retargeting buckets, and direct them into your funnels.

2. Invest in Google & Bing Ads.

As I said earlier in this chapter, only 5% out of your website's traffic is typically going to be in buying mode. Targeting that 5% of prospects that are in buying mode is generally fairly straightforward. They are immediately hungry and willing to explore the first options presented to them. We want our advertising to appear as immediate in their search process as possible.

In this case, it is best to use search ads, as search engines will traditionally be the avenue that they'll be using to conduct their search and the best avenue for capturing warm search traffic. These search ads should be an active component of your marketing strategy.

When it comes to driving as much heavily targeted traffic to your sales funnel and initiatives as possible, Google and Bing ads are the most effective options available. There are plenty of benefits here, but being able to target search users who are currently searching for specific keywords related to your key activities provides you with a wonderful opportunity to achieve better conversion rates on your ads.

Unlike other forms of marketing that place your ad in front of passive buyers, your ads in Google and Bing show up when people are actively searching for that topic, so they are more likely and ready to engage.

Because the majority of internet browsers are only in the research process, they need access to more reliable content and information. If you follow our example of how to create effective search ads from earlier in this Secret, you'll be using your ads to sell access to information that you can provide, and your ads will definitely stand out from the crowd and have a higher click-through rate than your competitors.

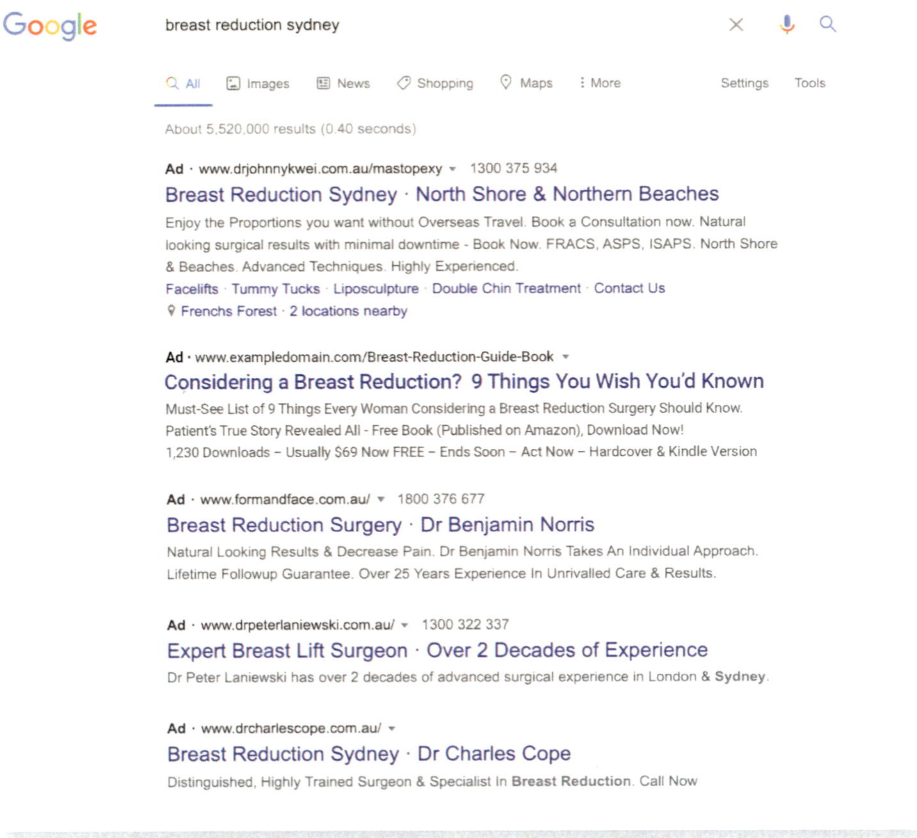

Figure 26: Make sure your ads generate curiosity

Some additional helpful tips for running effective Google and Bing Ads; target keywords related to the material that you are providing access to, and ensure that your attention-grabbing content title and a strong call-to-action show up in the second headline and the description copy of your ads respectively.

Even though Bing only accounts for 12.18%[11] of total internet search traffic at this time (Google has a 73.34% market share), you shouldn't

11 www.smartinsights.com/search-engine-marketing/search-engine-statistics/

leave any opportunity to drive targeted traffic to your content off the table, as you only pay by the click, making Bing ads just as effective as Google ads.

3. Search Engine Optimization

Search Engine Optimization (SEO), is the process where we get pages from your website (such as the landing page for your new book) better ranked in Google and other search engines, getting you more visibility and increased traffic.

Now, I could have listed this as a FREE technique, as one of the main benefits here is that you don't have to pay Google or any other search engine to get a better ranking. And once you are better ranked, you are gaining free clicks that you are hopefully converting on your landing page. Organic search traffic is wonderful and free.

But, the process of getting your pages better-ranked does take time and effort, and for that it generally involves money; mainly because it will be just more efficient for you to pay someone else to do it for you.

The modern techniques for improving your website's SEO are always changing, and unless you are staying up to date on those changes, you will need help with this. You don't need to know all of the details—your time is better served in building your practice.

But there are many things that you can do to help set a good base for your SEO. First, make sure that you feature the content's landing page prominently on your website, with additional relevant internal links from other pages if possible.

In regards to copy, include your content's title in the meta-title of the landing page and write a benefit-driven description for your meta-description with a strong call-to-action included in it.

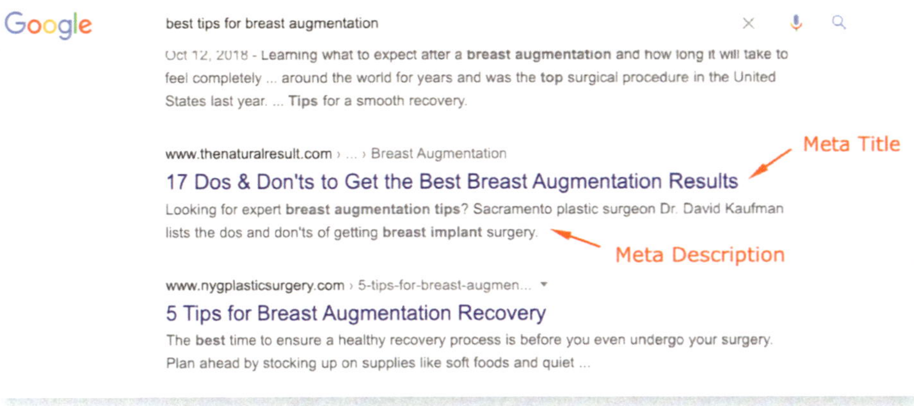

Figure 27: Display of the Meta Title and Meta Description of a web page in search results

Speed matters, so your website's content should load quickly. You can use Google's Pagespeed Insight[12] or GTMetrix[13] to analyse your website's speed. You can help make your website pages lighter by optimizing any images and videos before loading them onto your website. And as web traffic on mobile devices continues to increase, you should optimize your website's display, functionality and speed for mobile devices too.

And finally, keep all of your main necessary information within the users' initial view ("above the fold"), especially on mobile devices. Don't make people search long and hard to find key information, registration details or how to keep engaging with your practice.

12 www.developers.google.com/speed/pagespeed/insights/
13 www.gtmetrix.com/

Figure 28: Example of the initial mobile view for a book offer landing page. All key details appear "above-the-fold".

Alternatively, I can show you a quick shortcut to get you top of search results exposure while waiting for your organic ranking to climb to the top of page one on Google search results.

Look at page one of Google search results using your dream keywords, find any site that is not your competitors or sites that don't accept advertising, and outreach to them and ask them if they can feature your book as a banner or a link in an article that ranks highly on their search results.

By doing this, you can start getting traffic immediately from the sites that are currently ranking in those top positions. Your goal in the short-term isn't to outrank them; it is just to get eyes and leads towards your book funnels on their pages.

You will quickly realise how much more valuable a click to your lead magnet is from one of these pages, more so than even the same from Google's search results page. For example, this would be their three-step process for clicking towards you;

1. Typed in a phrase into Google
2. Clicked on a website in the displayed search results where you got a link displayed
3. Saw and clicked onto the link to your lead magnet funnel

The first click in Google is typically from the "browsers", but that second click comes from people who are much more serious: the buyers. Because they've made two clicks to get to you, they are much more likely to convert when they do get to your page.

Tons of the clicks that hit Google's search results are for general keywords that will be wasted on people who aren't serious, and if you're paying for these clicks, it can be expensive. That's why with the Google and Bing ads strategy I mentioned previously, I advised you to go for more specific keywords. But for general, broad keywords, it is best to buy your way in through advertising on the top-ranking websites already, as the people who have to click twice to get to you are the ones who are the most serious and will be worth the most money to you long-term.

In the very early sections of this book, I helped you identify your target audience and where they are hanging out online already, so you can reach out to those website owners to see what your advertising options are with them.

If they have an email newsletter, you can ask them if you can purchase a solo ad to their email list. If they have banner ads on their website, you can ask them how much it would cost to purchase a banner ad. If they have Google AdSense on their site (meaning they let Google run ads on their websites), then you can add their site to your list to target later using Google Display Network (GDN), through the Google Ads platform.

Getting links to your website on websites that are already ranked for your dream keywords is one of the fastest ways to get super qualified traffic to your website.

4. YouTube Ads

YouTube ads are a cheap and effective way for you to get a lot of views for your video content. Please also note that YouTube is owned by Google so you can set up your video ads using the same Google ads platform you've been using already.

YouTube ads are great, as users have to watch your video for a few seconds before they can skip to continuing watching their original intended video. You can fit a lot of great sellable and engaging content in those few seconds to help keep people interested, even after they have the opportunity to skip on by.

For building an effective campaign, you need to go back to your Dream 100 list of the people, brands, and influencers that your target audience is following, and find the relevant YouTube channels that are relevant to that list.

One of my favourite YouTube shortcuts is to find videos that are getting a lot of views, but where the creators of the videos don't really understand how to make money from their views. You can reach out to these people and ask them to feature your book or other links to desired content in their video descriptions, or you could pay people to create a video and post it on their channel for you. You could even pay them to let you put a playlist of a video series (about the procedure that you want to get known for) on their channel. The ideas and opportunities are endless!

You can use paid YouTube ads to place your ads on top of the other videos that are ranked for your dream keywords and the videos of your Dream 100 list.

To get the most out of your YouTube ads, it's important to follow these tips;

- Keep your video ads relatively short. Keep in mind that people are coming to YouTube to watch alternate content, and most people won't have the patience for a five-minute advertisement.
- Make sure to hook your audience quickly, as you will only have a few seconds to impress them before they have the option to hit that "Skip Ad" button.
- Insert a call-to-action button at the end screen of the video and include a link to the landing page on the website in the video description.

- Move prospective leads into your retargeting buckets, so we can turn them into traffic that we own, and then we will ascend them up to your value ladder (Special Offer Sign Up — Initial Consultation — Surgery Booking).

5. Influencer, Affiliate Partner Outreach

When done right, harnessing the power of social influencers, affiliate and referral partners can drive incredible awareness of your expertise in your niche, increasing engagement and patient enquiries. The key here is finding the people and referrals that your profiled typical patient follows and trusts.

Your network of affiliates can help you reach thousands or even millions of your desired target audience. Instead of just relying on your own email list, what if you found 10, 20 or 100 affiliates who each had an email list of tens of thousands of people, you could quickly reach millions!

The amount of leverage you get when you build an affiliate program and leverage the efforts of other people is huge.

When you find those people and places, your work effort is centred on trying to get those people and places to mention, review or promote you, your work and/or your practice.

For example, now that you have this great new book from Secret #1, you can use that book to reach out to social media influencers, affiliate partners or your referring doctors, and ask them to feature your book on their website, newsletter or in social media posts.

Shout-Outs From Social Media Influencers

With social media networks, you can quickly gain quality traffic to your funnels by getting a "shout-out" from high-profile social media influencers. For example, using your book as the lead magnet, these influencers could post a picture of themselves with your book, telling their audience a story about the book and its impact on them, then tagging you to give their audience a quick easy way to find you.

You can approach people personally to do these paid shout outs, but there are also a lot of agencies that specialise in getting shout-outs for you. You can hire them, and they'll do all the work to find the people, get you the shout out, and get people to your social media profile pages.

Facebook Messenger and Desktop Push

Currently, I don't know how many people are selling ads to their Messenger lists, but I do think that this market will start to grow. Because Messenger doesn't allow you to send obvious promotional content to your subscribers, the open and click-through rates on messages that are sent are second to none. I recommend finding people in your Dream 100 who are actively building Messenger lists and asking them if you can buy ads in their lists.

The same is true with desktop push notifications. This is a newer type of list that is getting a lot of traction right now. We're starting to build up a Dream 100 list of people in our market who are building up these lists so we can purchase broadcasts from them.

Mailing Campaign

Think about your Dream 100 list and see if there are opportunities to send direct mail campaigns to their buyer lists. Sometimes it's harder to get them to block out the time to send an email, but most of them aren't sending anything to their customers in the mail. You can set up deals with them where they send their customers' shipping addresses to a secure mailing house, so you never actually get access to their addresses, while you send a pre-approved mail content to that mailing house. The mailing house will then print your content, and then send it to the customer buyer list.

Facebook Groups and Forum Sites

Look out for additional promotional opportunities in your Dream 100 list. Within this list, see if there are any Facebook groups or forum sites where you can pay for a sponsored post or banner ad on their sites or groups.

SMS Campaign

As I mentioned earlier, SMS marketing is on the rise, you can ask your Dream 100 list to see if they have built a text message list so you can buy a text blast from them.

Blogging Sites and Their Pop-Ups

Most blogs in your market will sell ad space on their sites. Some have big Google AdSense blocks, banner ad areas that are reserved for Google Display ads, and I'll test my ads there initially using the Google Display Ads network to see if the ads convert well. If they do, I'll go directly to the blog or website owners and try to pay them to replace that text block with my banner ad exclusively, so that my ad will display on their blog on a full-time basis, not intermittently with Google Display Ads.

You can even pay people for a website pop up so that every reader to a blog can see messaging towards your clinic. You could also ask them for an exit pop-up placement, a pop-up that shows when readers are about to exit a website so that you can tap into the traffic that is leaving their websites and send them to you instead.

There is an unlimited number of ways to get in front of your Dream 100 audience's digital feeds. There are so many fun and creative things you can do, your imagination is really your only limitation. The key is to keep your eyes open for streams of traffic and distribution channels that people own; then figure out how to buy ads in them, drive traffic to your funnels and convert this traffic into traffic of your own.

Incentivising Your Affiliates

Depending on how well you can negotiate any ad placement deals with your affiliates and social media influencers, you can offer them an incentive for them to promote your offerings harder by offering money for each lead that they generate for you. For example, offering a flat $20 bonus for every book sign up that they generate for your book funnel.

From this, they will keep promoting your offers on an ongoing basis, instead of one-off campaigns because of this.

How much to give away per lead would be up to you. But you should understand your costs of new client acquisition, the lifetime value of a client, as well as the cost that you'd pay to other channels such as Google and Facebook ads to get engagement, for knowing what number is right for you.

Building a successful affiliate program has brought us more traffic, leads, and sales than any other marketing technique. If you pay your dues with your Dream 100, recruit them to be an affiliate, treat them well, and always figure out more ways to make them money, they will keep your funnels filled with your dream patients.

It's a guerrilla technique that works no matter what is happening with other major distribution channels like Facebook or Google; though you can still drive traffic to your funnels and generate more enquiries through them too.

If I turned off all other traffic techniques that we've been using and I only use these affiliate techniques, I'd still have an army of people buying Facebook Ads for me, sending out emails for me, ranking websites, and buying ads. Make this a priority and it will serve your practice for years.

Pro tip: Track using Google Analytics, where traffic to your landing page and website are coming from to judge whether a paid referral site is generating you the desired return on investment or not.

Some other helpful tips on using referral websites; make sure you get the optimal dimensions for any imagery that you can use on the referring website. Never let the referral website make your imagery for you without being able to approve it first.

And finally, don't forget to track the mentions of you, your practice and content by using Google Alerts[14]. Google Alerts is a content

14 https://www.google.com.au/alerts

detection and notification service offered by Google. The service sends emails to a user when it finds new results—such as web pages, newspaper articles, blogs, or scientific research—that match the user's search terms. This can be very helpful for understanding what people and networks are saying about your work.

As we mentioned earlier, there are many additional paid opportunities that we didn't talk about; from print marketing to TV, radio and streaming. All of these could have some benefit to you if your resources allow you to explore these avenues.

But while any form of marketing has the potential to bring in another new patient to your clinic, it is these 5 methods that will be your best most cost-effective high-traffic opportunities, so I wouldn't recommend exploring any other method until you've had a chance to nail down these specific techniques.

Once you have these in place, you'll be in a much better place for gauging whether you should be exploring other opportunities as well.

Remember, with every dollar you make online through these promotional channels, reinvest a big percentage of your profits back into advertising. And finally… don't stop! Traffic is the lifeblood of any company or clinic, and consistent lead flow is the secret to a healthy business.

"Sales is the oxygen of the clinic; nothing happens and no money is earned until something is booked or sold."

HUYEN TRUONG

SECRET #6: IMPROVE YOUR SALES PROCESS

Are you noticing other clinics offering similar services and procedures to you that only produce average clinical results compared to your industry-leading results? However, they seem to do very well with their marketing and sales, and prospective patients are just drawn to them.

We all know that a McDonald's burger isn't the tastiest one in the world, but they sell the most burgers in the world.

So, how do they do that?

Over my nearly 20 years of business consulting, I've been able to determine that the key factor for any successful business is how **they market & sell their products & services**. Period.

You might be extremely proud of the services that you offer, but the reality is that **nothing happens and no money is earned until something is booked (or sold).**

Sales is oxygen for a business; if you don't have sales, nothing else matters. Sales don't have to be pushy or sleazy; that is in fact an old-school tactic that just doesn't work anymore.

Are you with me on this?

Let me guess… you've been spinning your wheels, playing the sales "cat & mouse" game, speaking with prospects who at first sound interested, but then go cold, and you can't even get them back onto the phone, let alone get them to "pull the trigger" and actually book.

And you've spent countless time and money advertising more, pushing your message further out there hoping to catch more fish, with little to no result? All this time ignoring the one aspect that is probably hurting you the most.

Your sales process.

You might not even be aware that you should have a well-defined sales process in your clinic. But because you are likely selling mid-to-high priced luxury items such as consultations, treatments, and surgeries, this requires a serious proven sales process designed to convert more prospective patients into bookings.

And the reality is, that the majority of clinics out there right now have no idea what a good sales process looks like.

One of the key systems that I often see missing from a lot of clinics in their lead generating activities, is an effective sales process. Sales today is all about effective communication; convincing prospective patients to take the desired action on a service or product that you offer that provides value to them.

In order for your practice to grow quickly, you need to equip your key team members with great sales skills. This can include your receptionist, practice manager, patient coordinator, associates, and even other doctors.

Because these team members have certain touchpoints with prospective patients and existing patients, in order for your practice to sell well, you need to make sure that they are all well-equipped with great sales skills so that they can not only drive new patients to your clinic but also maintain existing patient relationships and gain referrals from them.

If you train them well, they should be able to do 70% of the selling and persuasion; the remaining 30% will be dependent on you or other associate doctors who see these new patients during the initial consultation process.

I have talked to many successful practice owners, and their practice managers or patient coordinators have helped them a lot by getting patients ready and keen for signing up even before meeting for their initial consultations.

Improving their sales skills and your sales process can improve your new patient conversion rate dramatically.

So, my question for you is: Does your clinic have a proven sales process in place to increase new patient enquiries that convert into actual bookings?

If not, you are in luck. I have taken all of my experiences interviewing successful practices on their best marketing and sales techniques, and I combined it with my own personal experiences selling

high-valued services over the last 10+ years, including all of my sales training, strategies and tactics, and I've documented all of it in my signature sales guide called *The 7-Figure Samurai Sword Sales Guide For Clinics.*

This is a crucial guide for practices. Not only does it save you hours of research and trial and error, but in it, I have created the ultimate proven sales process and system for your clinic, that will increase the new patient conversation rate at your practice.

Too often practices focus on the marketing side for generating more new business when there is a wealth of new bookings just waiting to be discovered simply by improving the quality of your sales process for your existing enquiries.

Improving your sales process isn't complicated. And it doesn't even have to be handled by you. But it does need to be clearly defined and properly established for it to be successful.

The 7-Figure Samurai Sword Sales Guide For Clinics is a must-read for businesses and practice owners looking for that key missing ingredient for generating more new bookings at their practice.

I can't cover all of the material here, in this book, but if you've ever doubted the quality of your sales process or want to learn more about how you can improve yours, you'd be well advised to give this sales guide a read.

I'll leave a link to a video in the Bonus section below that will demonstrate exactly what is included in the sales guide.

Improving your sales process is the final secret in a process that I've detailed in this book, that can turn you and your clinic into the trusted go-to celebrity authority in your selected niche.

I've covered a lot of ground here, outlined a clear actionable plan and the strategies that need to be taken to achieve it. The next step though is up to you.

So, what are you waiting for?

You have all you need to unleash your full potential towards the new patient generation. Honestly.

If you need more help, I've detailed an extensive bonus section of key tools that you can use to support you in your efforts, check it out.

And if you still have some questions, or need some help, let's talk… +61 2 91917388. Or email me at hello@queenofcosmeticmarketing.com.

Otherwise, the ball is now in your court.

I look forward to hearing your stories of success, as you implement the strategies in this book.

*"Focus does not mean saying yes;
it means saying no."*

STEVE JOBS

"MAKE YOUR LIFE EASIER" BONUSES

Because you are still reading this, I can let you in on a little bonus secret.

I've learnt that it is often the little things that get in the way of getting the really big things done. And because of that, I've also learnt some great ways to get those little things done without it turning into a time-wasting all-consuming exercise.

Getting those small little things out of the way will allow you to breathe again and move on to those more important bigger things that matter.

Like writing that book...

Outsource Your Bottleneck Away

Extraordinary results happen only when you are able to focus and concentrate on what's most important to you. Multitasking dilutes your focus and your results.

When we try to do everything, we end up with nothing. We jump from one small thing to the next, never fully accomplishing the key thing that we actually need to achieve.

Your time is worth money. Imagine the money you could be earning, if you were fully booked performing all the procedures you desired to handle in a month. How much money would you be earning per hour in such a scenario?

Every hour you waste on time-killing tasks that could have gone towards earning money performing procedures is money that could have been otherwise better spent freeing up your time and energy.

This means that you don't do your own social media. Don't edit your own photos and videos. Delegate your tasks as you need to, like invoices, graphic design, advertising, building website content, etc. The list could go on and on; I'm sure that you could fill it quickly.

In fact, I'm going to suggest that you make that list of the items that fill your day and that you circle the tasks that you don't want to do or that you don't have time for. And also circle the tasks or projects that you believe would take you to the next level that you need to dedicate the utmost attention to.

The next thing I would like for you to do is to delegate some of the tasks that you don't have the time for, or that you don't want to do, to your practice manager or an assistant that have the skills to handle those tasks successfully. Or even consider hiring an eligible agency that specializes in those tasks that you are looking to cover. And whichever tasks you still have remaining that haven't been allocated to someone, outsource the rest to a high-quality virtual assistant.

Find An Amazing Virtual Assistant

Why hire a full-time local employee when, in most cases, all you need is a full-time virtual assistant?

A Virtual Assistant is someone who works remotely and can handle numerous assorted tasks for you. They cost between $600–900 USD a month, and they will take care of all those little things that prevent you from focusing and working on those major things that matter for growing and scaling your practice.

I would suggest that you consider hiring a full-time Virtual Assistant to help you coordinate all those unallocated tasks, and find other qualified part-time Virtual Assistants to help you with "one and done" projects which are more technical, such as editing and publishing, video editing, graphic design, etc.

Virtual Assistants can have a bad reputation, there are a lot of places offering these services around the world, and not all are created equally. If you can find some recommendations from people that you trust, there are some amazing ones out there that can be a great help.

I've heard from clients having good success with Virtual Assistants from the Philippines and Eastern Europe. Though each will have their own unique skill sets, so you should be clear about the specific needs that you want a Virtual Assistant to address, and ensure that it matches their work history.

I've been to Eastern Europe and love it there, everything is cheaper than the rest of Europe. People are highly skilled, especially with technical tasks. However, you will have to pay more than what you would pay for a Virtual Assistant in the Philippines if that is a consideration.

Here are some job sites that are useful for finding good Virtual Assistants;

Worldwide:

www.upwork.com
www.freelancer.com
www.fiverr.com

Philippines:

www.virtualstafffinder.com
www.onlinejobs.ph

Serbia:

www.poslovi.infostud.com

Romania:

www.ejobs.ro

Remember; it's not a matter of just picking and clicking. Like any hire, you will need to go through a screening process to ensure that you are hiring only the most competent of applicants.

Key Notes About Publishing a Book

If you are still concerned about the amount of time needed for publishing a book, a Virtual Assistant can be an excellent resource for handling all of the details around publishing.

Apply for an ISBN

You will need to apply for an International Standard Book Number (ISBN) for your book in your country, as it depends on where you are located. For example, search "applying for ISBN in the US" and you will find the relevant site in the United States for applying. Keep in mind that you want to get an ISBN for both print and e-publication, which you will need to get your book published on multiple sites.

In order for you to apply for an ISBN, you will need to prepare the following items for publishing;

- Author biography (one paragraph)
- One headshot
    - Book description (one to three paragraphs in length)
    - The publishing imprint name, the trim size, and the book details (black-and-white, colour, etc.)

Key Assistants For Book Publishing

Once you have your Virtual Assistant in place for helping take smaller tasks off your plate, this person can help coordinate the remaining details of publishing your book, by sourcing and coordinating with the final Key Assistants needed to complete your book publishing;

- Book cover designer: You will need to decide on the book dimensions you want to print in and provide the designer with the front, back, and side copy text and your headshot to be included. The three most popular book trim sizes are 5 x 8, 5.5 x 8.5, and 6 x 9 inches.
- Book typesetter: This person will help you format your book correctly so that it looks neat and well organized for easy reading on Kindle, epub, and in print. (Sometimes a book editor can also be the formatter at the same time.)
- Book editor: It is always good to get a few pairs of eyes on your book before it is published, to remove any spelling or grammatical errors in advance, and to provide feedback and insight into your writing.

- Book printer: You have two simple choices (www.kdp.amazon.com or www.ingramspark.com) for around $3 a book. You will need to decide if you prefer it to be printed in black-and-white or in colour; though printing in colour will cost you a lot more.
- Book distributor: This person will help you distribute your published book on different platforms (Amazon KDP and Ingram Spark).

If you need help in terms of introducing you to our network of book publishing assistants, please let me know via hello@queenofcosmeticmarketing.com, and I will send you our reliable, high-quality contact list.

The 7-Figure Samurai Sword Sales Guide For Clinics

As part of our goal to help practices improve their conversion rates from new patient enquiries, the Online Marketing for Doctors team has produced this unique sales guide for clinics called **The 7-Figure Samurai Sword Sales Guide For Clinics...**

www.onlinemarketingfordoctors.com/samurai-sales-guide

This guide will not only benefit you as a practice owner, but it will also benefit your team members tremendously.

With these newly developed sales skills, you will be able to convert more prospects, motivate your team, and effectively pitch your practice to referring doctors for sending new patients to you.

Like the making of a Samurai sword, we have gone through the laborious process of hammering out and "folding the metal" back onto itself, iterating this process over the years to forge the strongest and sharpest sales guide possible.

In this guide, we are going to show you:

- The importance of sales and why you should equip your team with great sales skills
- Key facilities you need to have in place to improve your conversion rates of new patient enquiries
- How to take control of the conversation with a prospective patient and sell like a doctor (which is a good thing!)
- How to address different objections, like:
    1. The Real vs Non-Real Objection
    2. Your Toughest Objection
    3. The Deadliest Objection of All
    4. Pre-Framing Objections
    5. Money Objections
    6. Partner Objections
    7. "I Need To Think About It" Objections
- The art of the effective follow-up process. Fortunes are made in the follow-up process, and a lot of practices don't have a proven process in place to make this work.

We are going to give your team the key follow-up rules and a follow-up blueprint that anyone can follow so you know when to follow-up, what to say during a follow-up, and the multi-modality ways of following-up so your team can build rapport with prospects and make them know, like, and trust you to be their only choice for a procedure or treatment.

And finally, with this sales guide, we are going to give you and your

"Unless you have a reliable, duplicatable, scalable and consistent way to bring potential customers in, you don't have a business, you have a hobby."

MARK CUBAN

team an actual sales script so that you can see how a conversation with potential prospects will typically unfold and how you can handle the different situations and challenges presented by prospective patients during these conversations.

It will provide you with the necessary answers and strategies that will keep your conversation working towards a positive sales conclusion.

Automated Webinar Sales Funnel

In this book, I have shown you how to dominate social and search platforms by marketing educational and engaging content; and webinars are a great example of high-quality educational and engaging content that can help you connect and build trust and confidence with prospective patients in as little as 40 minutes.

For anyone who wants to learn how to build and to run a webinar effectively, please consider taking this 5-hour online course created by the experienced team at Online Marketing For Doctors designed to equip you with all of the tools that you would need to build your own webinar sales funnel, called;

This course is packed with templates and easy to follow instructions that you or a future Virtual Assistant can use to put together your first online webinar quickly and easily. This course provides a complete A–Z blueprint for using webinars to promote your high-value services, fill your calendar with bookings, and quickly put your scaled-up profits on autopilot.

We have spent over 250 hours creating this jam-packed 5-hour online course for you, and the end result is **6 core modules** and a treasure trove of swipe files, checklists, cheat sheets and plug 'n' play templates that hold your hand through every step of the way. It's everything you need to achieve your first automated webinar.

One engaging and profitable webinar can change everything for you and your practice. By following the clear, step-by-step roadmap we have laid out for you in this course, you'll be amply rewarded with a flood of new IDEAL patients and clients crashing down your gates, with higher audience engagement, trust and loyalty.

An automated webinar is a pre-recorded video streamed in real-time, in which you educate or inform your audience on a particular topic. Unlike a seminar or live webinar where you still have to trade time for money, an automated webinar system removes you from having to run ongoing live events. It allows your audience to join from anywhere around the country, or even the world, joining at a time that is convenient for them.

A pre-recorded automatic webinar sales system can unlock automation and engagement to create scalability for your business. It allows you to teach potential prospects valuable information that solidifies you as an expert in your field. Automated webinars help you build the key "Know, Like, and Trust" factors in a short amount of time, which are critical in the human buying process psychology.

Use this online course today to start creating a creative, less 'salesy' approach to promoting your high-ticket items such as medical treatments or surgeries.

Click here[15] to watch the video we made that walks you through the course in more detail, including everything that comes in this jam-packed online course.

Other Useful Tools

Video Capturing Apps

VivaVideo

Audio Recording Apps

RODE Rec Le

Video Captioning Service

Rev.com

Before and After Video Creator

Before and After Pro Slider

15 www.onlinemarketingfordoctors.com/webinar-sales-funnel-course/

ABOUT AUTHOR HUYEN TRUONG, MBA

Hi, I'm Huyen Truong

I'm Australian. I have lived and worked on three different continents, but I was born and raised in Vietnam in a poor working-class family during the de-centralising economic period of the 1980s. It was very tough back then.

I have walked a path that few other entrepreneurs have.

My parents worked very hard juggling various business ventures just to put food on the table.

I learnt one valuable thing from my parents' success.

One word. **Persistence.**

Nothing in this world can take the place of good old persistence.

Talent won't.

Genius won't.

Education won't.

Persistence and determination are all-powerful.

They are the principles that enabled my parents to rise up in their lives when most people their age were giving up or thinking about retirement.

Growing up, I saw them trying many different types of businesses and opportunities until they finally experienced a breakthrough with one of their businesses when they were in their late 40s.

My parents had finally turned a small business into a multi-million dollar business. But it took a long time to get there.

It was in this humble beginning that inspired me to dream of a better future for myself, and I picked up my business sense from them.

I started selling candy for money when I was 5. I was trying to sell things around me as much as possible to make any extra cash I could to buy treats that my parents were unable to afford at the time. The entrepreneurial spirit inside of me was unleashed very early on, and I haven't looked back.

I even started selling online advertising in the early 2000s when online marketing was still in its infancy, as I knew back then it would be the future of marketing.

Through many years of working hard and saving money, my parents were able to send me to the United States for graduate education.

I graduated from the University of Missouri-Columbia with an MBA during one of the worst financial crises, 2008–2010.

But during that financial crisis, instead of choosing to stay in America and trying to survive there, I decided to make a bold move by packing my bags and moving to Australia. It's something none of my classmates even considered.

I moved to Australia in 2011 as a poor student without any connections, no job, money, or family and friends—just two suitcases and more than $100,000 in student debt.

I started out sharing a room with another student, living in a tiny old house with 8 other students, with no heater and just one bathroom to share. Every night, I could feel the cold, high-pitched whistling winds blowing through the rattling bedroom window, keeping me awake at night. Life didn't look so promising back then.

But I had this dream on the first day I stepped foot in Australia of creating a leading digital marketing agency, and that dream has kept me going until today.

Back then, I had no idea how to make it happen, but I just knew deep down that I was going to achieve it someday.

I started small, slowly building a reputation by working on multiple jobs helping small businesses with their search marketing. Result

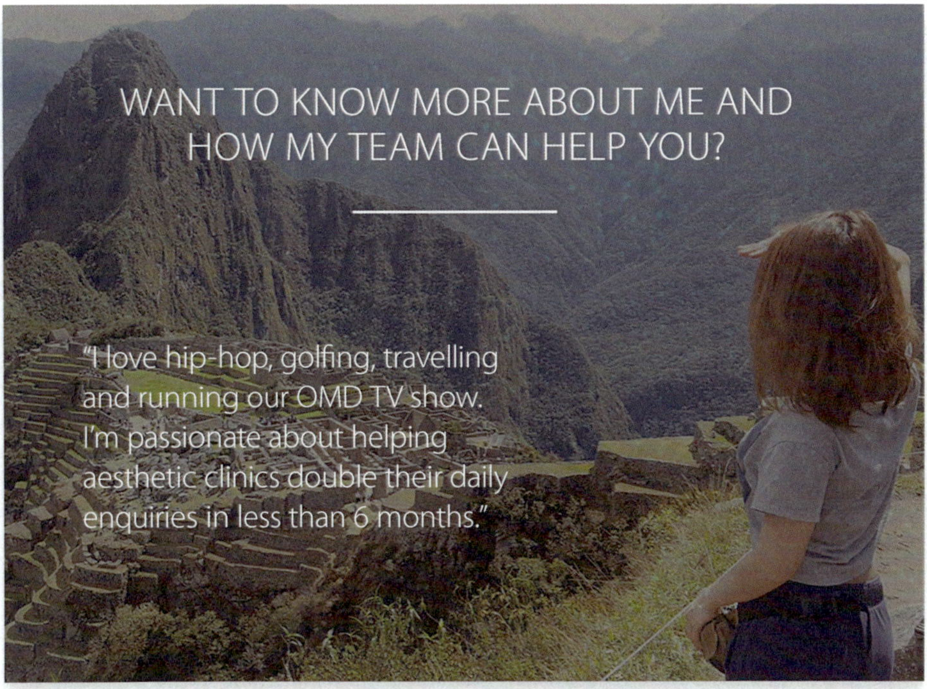

Driven SEO was the first agency I founded, and while it didn't happen overnight, it started growing bigger and bigger.

But it grew to a point when I realised that the competition in this broad industry was getting really fierce. The competition was everywhere, and everyone was chasing any potential client making any wild promise they could just to land them.

It was in those moments that I began to understand the value of specialising in one niche and how it could set my agency apart from my competitors. That's why I founded Online Marketing for Doctors (OMD) and Queen of Cosmetic Marketing, to claim my celebrity authority on a niche industry that I knew very well.

This company has since grown incredibly well over time, and I couldn't be prouder of the work that my wonderful OMD team has done to support cosmetic and plastic surgeons across Australia and around the world, to achieve their own dreams for their practices. It has been incredibly satisfying work.

But the tale doesn't end here. It is constantly being rewritten every day with new exciting challenges and opportunities in this dynamically changing and ever-growing industry. And I plan on continuing to push forward, striving to be the best that I can be, in the same fighting spirit that my wonderful parents instilled in me those many years ago.

Persistence.

ABOUT QUEEN OF COSMETIC MARKETING

One year after launching Online Marketing For Doctors and Queen of Cosmetic Marketing, my agency has experienced an incredible 166% growth rate. That's why I wanted to write this book, to show you the power of the niche.

Today, I'm leading a star team of digital marketers helping aesthetic clinics all over the world to double their new patient enquiries in less than 6 months.

I have a special interest in the aesthetic industry and an incredible passion in helping plastic surgeons from around the world to thrive and succeed with their clinics.

From reconstructive-turned-cosmetic surgeons to young, thriving plastic surgeons to world-renowned plastic surgeons or presidents of the Australasian and American Society of Aesthetic Plastic Surgeons, I have helped them all to succeed in online lead generation and build a strong and resilient brand in this hyper-competitive aesthetic industry.

I have built a dream team designed for building incredible aesthetic clinics' digital marketing campaigns. **You get to work with specialists, not generalists.**

We are a boutique team of 15 incredible talents, and we don't plan on expanding our team any time soon.

Why?

Because it's super hard to find similar talents that my team has and I don't work with just any clinic. I select a limited number of clinics in each city to work exclusively with so I can make sure that I personally set a strategy and follow through on the implementation, ensuring that you get unmatched dedication and attention from my team that doesn't compete against any of my other clients.

The quality and results of your campaign are second to none, as your success is our ultimate goal and the reason for our existence.

We are known by our clients for our four core qualities:

- Responsiveness
- Thoroughness
- Results Driven
- Proactive

We work hard to ensure that these qualities are carried throughout our working process with all of our clients.

I was lucky to meet Warren Buffet—billionaire and legendary investor—when I was doing my MBA in the USA, and he told us this;

"Someone's sitting in the shade today because someone planted a tree a long time ago." - Warren Buffet

Ever since then, I've always wanted to plant a tree, a tree of a proven marketing system and framework for cosmetic and plastic surgeons around the world that they can use, so that they can enjoy the benefits that come with successfully growing and scaling their practice.

If you are interested in speaking with me and my team, please book a call with us.

BOOK A STRATEGY CALL WITH QUEEN OF COSMETIC MARKETING TEAM

WHAT OTHER SURGEONS SAY ABOUT US

DR. HODGKINSON

Client's testimonial:
https://youtu.be/d_AhqfJ34wY

*"**The number of requests for consultations has at least doubled in the last five months, which is a very good sign.** We're very impressed with how much detail they put into the plan, how they projected what they might be able to achieve for us. I've enjoyed working with both principles. We look forward to the future, as right now the present is very positive for us."*

Dr Darryl Hodgkinson – MBBS (Honors II) FRCS (C), FACS, FACCS, Cosmetic & Plastic/Reconstructive Surgeon

DR. NAVEEN SOMIA

Client's testimonial:

www.youtube.com/watch?v=IvTJ4JStdvE

"What I saw was the ranking slowly starting to climb and we were very happy with the way the rankings were going, especially for some of the keywords that I wanted to be on the first page of Google.

That translated into a lot of visitors coming to my website. Over the ***last 12 months*** *we have increased* ***the web traffic by over 100% and also increased the conversions by 100%.***

And so far, I'm happy with the progress that we have made. And the one nice thing about Huyen is that every time she had the option to go with the more expensive version, she always recommended the cheaper version with the view of adding value to me as the client, which is very reassuring and a lot different from what my experiences have been in the past."

Dr Naveen Somia – MBBS, PhD, FRACS Cosmetic & Plastic/Reconstructive Surgeon/ ASAPS President

LUMIERE BEAUTY CLINIC

Client's testimonial:
https://youtu.be/F4vvStugS8M

"We've seen a ***significant increase in our website traffic and enquiries by over 300%****, with an obvious uptake in new patient enquiries and conversions coming through the clinic. We've seen a complete turnaround in our online presence in several spaces that we are advertising in."*

Christy Xuan - Owner/ Managing Director of Lumiere Beauty Clinic

PCLS COFFS HARBOUR

Client's testimonial:
https://youtu.be/TS8l4JW32dM

"They put together a comprehensive strategy and plan to improve our digital marketing presence (SEO, PPC ads, Website Content and Landing Pages), and so far ***we can see obvious improved results*** *from the work that they have done."*

Dr Chandran Arianayagam – Plastic Surgeon /Owner of PCLS Coffs Harbour

Chandran Arianayagam

CROWN CLINIC

We have been using the Online Marketing for Doctors team for ***almost 6 months now*** *and we are very happy with the results. They put together a comprehensive strategy and plan to improve our digital marketing presence (SEO, PPC ads, Social Media, Website Content and Landing Pages), and so far we can see obviously improved results from the work that they have done.* ***Enquiries have gone crazy and the number of enquiries has increased three-fold ever since they started.*** *The team and Huyen have been very responsive to support us along the way with our IT problems, they are very thorough and results-driven with their work. We would highly recommend them.*

James Nadin – CEO of ICCM & Crown Clinic

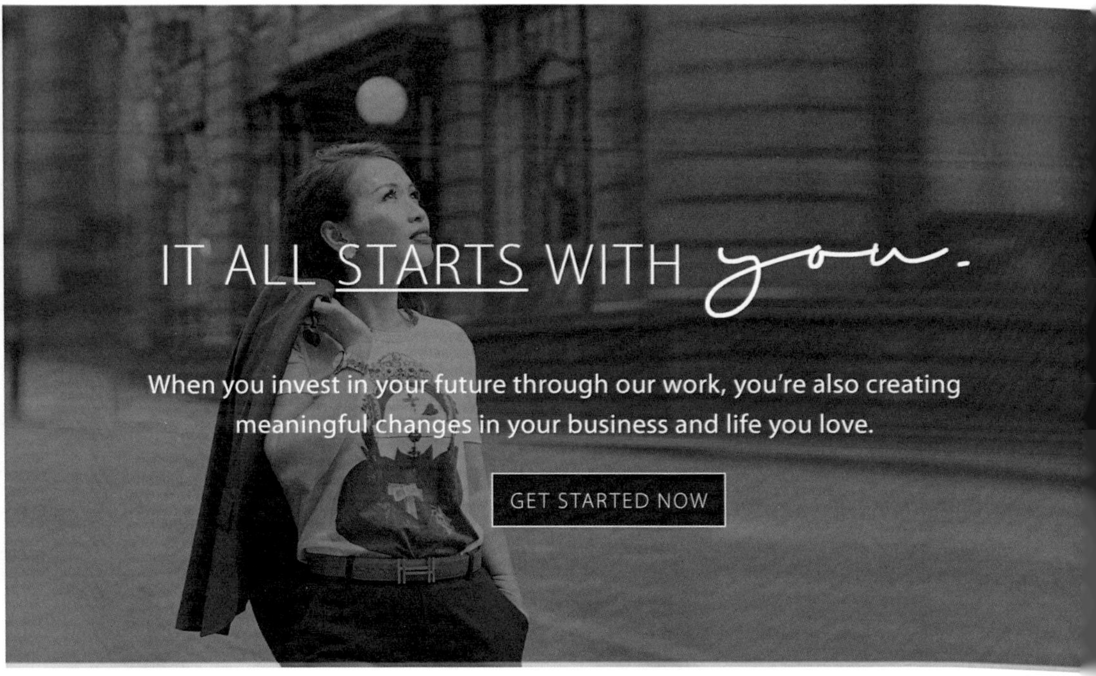
IT ALL STARTS WITH you.
When you invest in your future through our work, you're also creating meaningful changes in your business and life you love.
GET STARTED NOW